HOW to GET $50,000 WORTH OF BUSINESS SERVICES FREE
EACH YEAR from the UNITED STATES GOVERNMENT

AUTHOR OF

How I Made $1,000,000 In Mail Order

HOW TO GET $50,000 WORTH OF SERVICES *FREE,* EACH YEAR, FROM THE U.S. GOVERNMENT

By E. Joseph Cossman

A World of Books That Fill a Need

FREDERICK FELL INC.   New York

From time to time the author, E. Joseph Cossman, gives business seminars across the country. If you'd like to know when a seminar will be given in your city, you can get this information by writing to:

Mr. E. Joseph Cossman
P.O. Box 1066
Studio City, Calif. 91604

New Printing, 1972

Dedicated to My Father,

THEODORE H. COSSMAN

WHO, LIKE THOUSANDS OF OTHERS,
HAD THE COURAGE AND FORESIGHT TO LEAVE HIS NATIVE LAND
SO HIS CHILDREN COULD BE BORN AND RAISED
IN THIS WONDERFUL, WONDERFUL COUNTRY.

TABLE OF CONTENTS

HOW to GET $50,000 WORTH OF BUSINESS SERVICES FREE
EACH YEAR from the UNITED STATES GOVERNMENT

INTRODUCTION

A harassed farmer sat down one day and penned a letter:

"DEAR GOVERNMENT: Will you please tell me how to get rid of dandelions? I've tried everything."

Eventually he got his answer:

"DEAR SIR: We don't know of anything that will get rid of dandelions, but here's a great recipe for dandelion wine."

While Abraham Lincoln was still delivering the mail in his stovepipe hat, citizens were turning to Uncle Sam with their problems. Then, as now, Uncle was ready to help out, if he could; and if he couldn't, he could always suggest dandelion wine. When the mail got too heavy to answer in the friendly fashion above, form letters were substituted; and finally the present practice evolved of issuing publications on every subject an American citizen might be interested in.

Housewife, mariner, trout fisherman, or astronaut; chess player, rock hound, farmer, or mortician: whatever your interest, your Uncle Sam has valuable help and information for you. Much of it is yours for the asking. The rest is offered well under cost. The information in one publication alone, *General Social and Economic Char-*

acteristics, cost over $25,000 per page to compile. Yet this 214-page book is yours for only $1.25. Much of what you'll find in it is unavailable anywhere else.

Uncle Sam runs the largest publishing house in the world just for you. Created in 1860, the Government Printing Office turns out a staggering amount of material every year. There are over 1,250,000 titles in print, and more are pouring out at the rate of 20,000 annually.

All the material is carefully prepared by recognized experts in the field. It is as accurate, factual, and helpful as is humanly possible to make it.

Want to go into a new business? What are your chances for success? What's the best location? How much money do you need? The best stock to buy? You have a thousand such questions on your minds. To whom will you turn for help? You can't always trust suppliers, for they're eager to sell you their goods. You can't always trust real-estate agents, for they're anxious to rent you their property. You can't always trust your friends, for they are bent upon giving you sugar-coated advice just to keep you happy. And you certainly can't trust your competitors, for many of them would do anything to keep you out of business.

But Uncle Sam has nothing to sell you but help. He has no ax to grind, and his information is impartial and objective.

Looking for a new product to sell? Uncle Sam will tell you how to develop new products and give you lists of royalty-free inventions from which you may choose. (See Chapter III.)

Interested in running a business out of your own home? He's ready to help with solid, valuable information. (See Chapter I.)

Want to sell overseas? The Bureau of International Commerce will actually locate jobbers, dealers, agents for you in any country you can name. (See Chapter IV.)

Want to learn a language? The government offers manuals not only on French, Spanish, Italian, or German, but on Swahili, Urdu, Hindi! (See Chapter IX.)

Got an inventive mind? The role of the Patent Office is well known, but are you aware that the Department of Commerce publishes lists of inventions wanted by the Armed Forces and other government agencies? (See Chapter VI.)

Got something to sell? Uncle Sam can be your best customer. Moreover, the government issues regular lists of products wanted and continually solicits bids. Those lists are yours for the asking. (See Chapter VI.)

Got an idea that has commercial possibilities for some industry, yet can't be patented or copyrighted? How do you protect yourself? A lawyer's advice will cost you $50 or $100. The government charges less than a dollar for Annual No. 3 of *Management Aids for Small Business* which, among other valuable information, gives you rules for protecting an intangible but salable idea. (See Chapter V.)

Would you like Uncle Sam to grubstake you for a prospecting expedition? He'll do it! (See Chapter V.)

Want to know how to keep from losing your shirt in mail order? Ask Uncle. (See Chapter I.)

Ever dream of living on a lazy Bali H'ai type island of your own in the South Seas? Uncle will sell you one . . . cheap! (See Chapter V.)

Cutthroat competition getting you down? You don't have to go under. (See Chapter II.)

Would you like the President of General Motors to

represent your company abroad . . . at no charge? It could happen, if you asked for Uncle's free help from the right trade mission. (See Chapter IV.)

Like to bring customers into your store with a free movie every day? Uncle Sam shows you where to find them. (See Chapter V.)

Want to get the "red carpet" treatment when you travel to Europe . . . at no extra charge? It happened to me; it could happen to you! (See Chapter IV.)

Need art work or photographs for your advertising? The Library of Congress and the National Archives have probably ten million pictures on file. Virtually all Government agencies and departments in Washington take pictures of their activities and projects, whether it be building roads, counting fish, or firing earth satellites into space. They keep files of these and fill photo requests at very low prices. (See Chapter IX.)

Is foreign competition infringing on your trade-mark or copyright? You may call on the Treasury Department of the United States to prohibit the entry of such infringing foreign-made merchandise into this country. (See Chapter VIII.)

All right. What you've just read only scratches the surface of what your government is anxious to give to you for little or nothing. Nobody could tell it all. Even the government itself can't keep track of the flood of valuable and useful information and knowledge that spews out yearly from the Government Printing Office. The various government agencies try to keep on top of the flood with their own compiled lists, but it's almost impossible. However, because of the multitude of information that is gathered each day by the Government, it's safe to assume as a working rule:

IF THERE'S ANYTHING YOU WANT TO KNOW
ABOUT ANYTHING UNDER THE SUN, YOUR
GOVERNMENT PROBABLY HAS A PAMPHLET
ON IT!

These publications range from a single-page handout to a giant 1,036-page volume which in itself is a bibliography of government publications, modestly entitled, *Selected U.S. Government Publications*. SELECTED!

Does the public use this tremendous wealth of material? Well, the largest-selling book in the history of the United States is the government's brochure on *Infant Care*. It outsells the Bible. Eight and a half million copies have been distributed . . . so far.

A tremendous achievement? Perhaps. But when you consider that there are fifty million *mothers* in this country it becomes evident that the people who *don't* know how to use the government's resources far outnumber those who *do!*

The situation in relation to business is even worse. A dozen government agencies put out information vital to businessmen. That's where this book comes in. The volume you hold in your hand is unique. It pulls together all the *best* material from all agencies and sources for one purpose: to show the businessman the best that Uncle Sam has to offer him from every source. It gives you the big picture.

The purpose of this book is to acquaint you with the phenomenal variety, diversity, scope, and sheer *money value* that your Uncle Sam is begging you, as a consumer or as a businessman, to take advantage of. This book does not pretend to give an exhaustive list of the thousands of government resources at your fingertips for the asking, but it acts as a guide in directing you to these resources.

In addition to the publications, the pictures, the motion pictures (yes, the government agencies even have films on their activities which are available for your use), you will also learn of the services you can call upon for your own use as a citizen of the United States.

So you see, the title of this book is no exaggeration. As an American citizen, you *can* get $50,000 worth of business services *free* each year.

Your government *wants* you to take advantage of these services. This book tells you how and where to obtain them. The money you invested in this book is like taking a flier on an oil well . . . when you already know the gusher has come in! All you have to do is cash in.

Go to it!

Technical inquiries will be answered by the author if sent to the following address:

Mr. E. Joseph Cossman
Post Office Box 1066
Studio City, California, 91604

CHAPTER I

UNCLE SAM AS YOUR BUSINESS PARTNER

Starting Your Own Business with Government Help

SO YOU WANT TO GO INTO BUSINESS!

While the notion is still a gleam in your eye, you've already got yourself a partner: your Uncle Sam. He's a funny partner in some ways.

If you're successful, he takes part of the profits through taxes. If you're *more* successful, he takes *more* of the profits.

If you go into the red, he *doesn't* pay half the debts. Through his Collector of Internal Revenue, he will make some concessions. He'll allow you to offset your losses against your gains and forgo some or all of his share of the profits. He'll even let you balance the bad years against the good years, with limitations. But fork over cash to pay your creditors? No, sir. Some partner!

All right, that's the bad part. Comes to about half a page. For the next two hundred pages or so, you're going to hear about the *other* side of that partner of yours, the *good* side. Nobody's perfect, but how's that for percentage?

UNCLE OPENS THE DOOR . . .

I've yet to meet any red-blooded, employed male in this country who hasn't at one time or another expressed a strong desire to be in business for himself. It's not a case of the grass looking greener; it's a normal tendency to resist authority and strive for independence.

If you've been contemplating starting a business of your own, either part or full time, Uncle Sam has a staff of experts who can save you (and help you make) thousands of dollars in time and sound advice. You couldn't afford to pay for even a small percentage of the man-hours that have gone into the research and development material which these experts have gathered to help you. Hundreds of booklets, pamphlets, brochures, books, and folders are available, and they're yours. All you have to do is ask for them.

Just one *free* bulletin might be the key which could open the door to an entirely new career for you.

THERE'S A GOLD MINE WAITING TO BE TAPPED . . .

This book wasn't written to encourage you to go into business for yourself. It wasn't published to tell you the occupation you should pursue. Its main purpose is to expose you to the many aids available to you as a tax-payer and also to the thousands of publications which the United States Government publishes each year—books and literature on file which can help you make money and save money. Many are free, some cost 15 cents, some 30 cents, others 45 cents or 60 cents or more. Regardless of the price, you'll be rewarded time and again for the modest initial investment you make.

This probably sounds as though I'm conducting a one-man public-relations campaign for the Government Printing Office. Actually, I am. From past experience, using the methods I've outlined in this book, I've had such great personal success in my business that I'd like to share them with others. I had to learn this information the hard way; all you have to do is follow a few simple instructions, and you'll have more material at your fingertips than you could gather in any other manner.

IT'S YOUR DECISION . . .

Let's say you agree with me that you want to go into business for yourself. Fine; but remember this cliché, because it's one of the most important suggestions I can give you:

Don't tell anyone at your present place of employment that you're thinking about opening your own shop, store, or business. It's really a personal matter: your own. Don't tell your friends. Word gets out, and the first thing you know you may be looking for a job months before you're ready to make the big plunge. Unless you are independently wealthy, it's sound advice to stay with one job until you are definitely set to move to another. This may sound elementary, but I've seen too many men with ideas which were nothing more than pipe dreams get kicked in the teeth because they were unprepared when they started "on their own."

EASY DOES IT . . .

Walk before you run. Find out all you can about the job opportunities in the business you have selected. Just remember, and take heart: probably nowhere else has Uncle knocked himself out more to help as much as he helps the businessman . . . you.

If this surprises you, if you haven't seen any of this help around, believe me, it's *your* fault, not his. Uncle Sam conducts the biggest printing plant in the world— the Government Printing Office—and from it he pours out floods of valuable material to assist you in every possible phase of your business life.

And right here I want to introduce you to a man who can become the greatest business contact you'll ever make. He's the man to see about the hundreds of government publications I'm going to tell you about in this book as well as the hundreds of thousands of other publications put out by the GPO. Whenever you're in doubt about how to get any of the books, magazines, leaflets, and booklets from any department of the government, you can write to: *Superintendent of Documents, U.S. Government Printing Office, Washington, D.C. 20402.* He'll have it, and he'll send it to you.

HELP IS ON THE WAY! . . .

A large proportion of the material is aimed at guiding you right from the very start of your business. The reason? Businesses fail. Failures are bad for the individual, for those around him, and for the country in general. Uncle *wants* you to succeed. And short of leading you by the hand through every step of the way, he's going to do what he can to put you into the happy roster of successful, profit-making businessmen.

YOUR FRIEND, THE DEPARTMENT OF COMMERCE . . .

Many departments and agencies of the government help the businessman, but the Department of Commerce (as you can tell from its name) is by far your best source of help in the business field. About half of the publications I'll be bringing to your attention in succeeding chapters come from that department. On the next page you'll see a list of the department's Field Offices. If one of them is near you, go in and get acquainted. I think your eyes will be opened.

Many of the publications you'll want will be available in the Field Office, so you can save time by asking there before you bother the busy superintendent in Washington.

Also, certain libraries are designated as depositories for government publications. The Superintendent sends them all, or almost all, of the government publications as they come out. The list of the more than four hundred libraries is too long to give here, but if you ask for the *United States Department of Commerce Publications, 1963 Supplement* (25 cents), you'll find the depository libraries listed. If one is in your city, you will be able to use it to save time and expense by borrowing or consulting the library's files.

Another name you're going to come across constantly in these pages is the Small Business Administration. The SBA is the first independent agency of the federal government ever established in peacetime solely to advise and assist the nation's small business concerns. This agency, too, has regional and branch offices throughout the country, so use the one nearest you to save time. The list is given below.

If you have occasion to go to Washington on business, make your first stop the department's headquarters at 14th and "E" streets. There's a Business Service Center there where a business analyst who knows his way around will direct you to the official and agency you'll need to see to complete your business quickly and properly.

Department of Commerce Field Offices

Alburquerque, New Mexico 87101
U.S. Courthouse
Area Code 505 Tel. 247-0311

Anchorage, Alaska 99501
306 Loussac-Sogn Building
Area Code 907 Tel. 272-6331

Atlanta, Georgia 30303
4th Floor Home Savings Building
75 Forsyth Street N.W.
Area Code 404 Tel. 526-6000

Baltimore, Maryland 20212
305 U.S. Customhouse
Gay and Lombard Streets
Area Code 301 Tel. 962-3560

Birmingham, Alabama 35205
Suite 200-201
908 S. 20th Street
Area Code 205 Tel. 325-3327

Boston, Massachusetts 02203
Room 510
John Fitzgerald Kennedy Federal
    Building
Area Code 617 Tel. 233-2312

Buffalo, New York 14203
504 Federal Building
117 Ellicott Street
Area Code 716 Tel. 842-3208

Charleston, South Carolina 29403
Federal Building, Suite 631
334 Meeting Street
Area Code 803 Tel. 577-4171

Charleston, West Virginia 25301
3002 New Federal Office Building
500 Quarrier Street
Area Code 304 Tel. 343-6196

Cheyenne, Wyoming 82001
6022 Federal Building
2120 Capitol Avenue
Area Code 307 Tel. 634-5920

Chicago, Illinois 60604
1486 New Federal Building
219 South Dearborn Street
Area Code 312 Tel. 353-4400

Cincinnati, Ohio 45202
8028 Federal Office Building
550 Main Street
Area Code 513 Tel. 684-2944

Cleveland, Ohio 44114
Room 600
666 Euclid Avenue
Area Code 216 Tel. 522-4750

Dallas, Texas 75202
Room 1200
1114 Commerce Street
Area Code 214 Tel. 749-3287

Denver, Colorado 80202
16419 Federal Building
20th and Stout Streets
Area Code 303 Tel. 297-3246

Des Moines, Iowa 50309
609 Federal Building
210 Walnut Street
Area Code 515 Tel. 284-4222

Detroit, Michigan 48226
445 Federal Building
Area Code 313 Tel. 226-6088

Greensboro, North Carolina 27402
258 Federal Building
W. Market Street
P.O. Box 1950
Area Code 919 Tel. 275-9111

Hartford, Connecticut 06103
18 Asylum Street
Area Code 203 Tel. 244-3530

Honolulu, Hawaii 96813
286 Alexander Young Building
1015 Bishop Street
Tel. 588-977

Houston, Texas 77002
5102 Federal Building
515 Rusk Avenue
Area Code 713 Tel. 228-0611

Jacksonville, Florida 32202
P.O. Box 35087
400 W. Bay Street
Area Code 904 Tel. 791-2796

Kansas City, Missouri 64106
Room 2011
911 Walnut Street
Area Code 816 Tel. 374-3141

Los Angeles, California 90015
Room 450
Western Pacific Building
1031 S. Broadway
Area Code 213 Tel. 688-2833

Memphis, Tennessee 38103
710 Home Federal Building
147 Jefferson Avenue
Area Code 901 Tel. 534-3214

Miami, Florida 33130
Room 821
City National Bank Building
25 W. Flagler Street
Area Code 305 Tel. 350-5267

Milwaukee, Wisconsin 53203
Straus Building
238 W. Wisconsin Avenue
Area Code 414 Tel. 272-8600

Minneapolis, Minnesota 55401
306 Federal Building
110 S. Fourth Street
Area Code 612 Tel. 334-2131

New Orleans, Louisiana 70130
909 Federal Office Building, S.,
610 South Street
Area Code 504 Tel. 527-6546

New York, New York 10007
41st Floor
Federal Office Building
26 Federal Plaza
Area Code 212 Tel. 264-0634

Philadelphia, Pennsylvania 19107
Jefferson Building
1015 Chestnut Street
Area Code 215 Tel. 597-2850

Phoenix, Arizona 85025
5413 New Federal Building
230 N. First Avenue
Area Code 602 Tel. 261-3285

Pittsburgh, Pennsylvania 15222
2201 Federal Building
1000 Liberty Avenue
Area Code 412 Tel. 644-2850

Portland, Oregon 97204
217 Old U.S. Courthouse
520 S.W. Morrison Street
Area Code 503 Tel. 226-3361

Reno, Nevada 89502
2028 Federal Building
300 Booth Street
Area Code 702 Tel. 784-5203

Richmond, Virginia 23240
2105 Federal Building
400 N. 8th Street
Area Code 703 Tel. 649-3611

St. Louis, Missouri 63103
2511 Federal Building
1520 Market Street
Area Code 314 Tel. 622-4243

Salt Lake City, Utah, 84111
3235 Federal Building
125 S. State Street
Area Code 801 Tel. 524-5116

San Francisco, California 94102
Federal Building
Box 36013
450 Golden Gate Avenue
Area Code 415 Tel. 556-5864

San Juan, Puerto Rico 00902
Room 100
Post Office Building
Phone 723-4640

Savannah, Georgia 31402
235 U.S. Courthouse and Post Office Building
125-29 Bull Street
Area Code 912 Tel. 232-4321

Seattle, Washington 98104
809 Federal Office Building
909 First Avenue
Area Code 206 Tel. 583-5615

Small Business Administration Offices Are Located in the Following Cities:

Agana, Guam
Alburquerque, New Mexico
Anchorage, Alaska
Atlanta, Georgia
Augusta, Maine
Baltimore, Maryland
Birmingham, Alabama
Boise, Idaho
Boston, Massachusetts
Buffalo, New York
Casper, Wyoming
Charleston, West Virginia
Charlotte, North Carolina
Chicago, Illinois
Cincinnati, Ohio
Clarksburg, West Virginia
Cleveland, Ohio
Columbia, South Carolina
Columbus, Ohio
Concord, New Hampshire
Dallas, Texas
Denver, Colorado
Des Moines, Iowa
Detroit, Michigan
Dover, Delaware
Fairbanks, Alaska
Fargo, North Dakota
Harlingen, Texas
Hartford, Connecticut
Hato Rey, Puerto Rico
Helena, Montana
Honolulu, Hawaii
Houston, Texas
Indianapolis, Ind.
Jackson, Mississippi
Jacksonville, Florida
Kansas City, Missouri
Knoxville, Tennessee
Las Vegas, Nevada

Little Rock, Arkansas
Los Angeles, California
Louisville, Kentucky
Lubbock, Texas
Madison, Wisconsin
Marquette, Michigan
Marshall, Texas
Miami, Florida
Milwaukee, Wisconsin
Minneapolis, Minnesota
Montpelier, Vermont
Nashville, Tennessee
Newark, New Jersey
New Orleans, Louisiana
New York, New York
Oklahoma City, Oklahoma
Omaha, Nebraska
Philadelphia, Pennsylvania
Phoenix, Arizona
Pittsburgh, Pennsylvania
Portland, Oregon
Providence, Rhode Island
Richmond, Virginia
St. Louis, Missouri
St. Thomas, Virgin Islands
Salt Lake City, Utah
San Antonio, Texas
San Diego, California
San Francisco, California
Seattle, Washington
Sioux Falls, South Dakota
Spokane, Washington
Syracuse, New York
Tampa, Florida
Toledo, Ohio
Tucson, Arizona
Washington, D. C.
Wichita, Kans.

For addresses and telephone numbers of the SBA Field Offices listed above, consult the appropriate telephone directory.

Both in Washington and in the regional offices you'll be almost embarrassed by the help the government consultant offers you. Often he will make a visit to your store, plant, or proposed location to give you on-the-spot advice.

A thrifty tip: while much of the government printed material is free (and I stand by the title of this book absolutely!), a lot more is available at the cost of printing, which may range from a dime to several dollars. I've found, though, that if you pick up the books in the Field Offices of SBA, the Department of Commerce, or the other agencies we'll talk about later in this book, the man will usually hand them to you without charge. So, if it's not too much of a trip, drop in on the Field Office and use the Superintendent of Documents only when the Field Office is out of reach or out of stock.

WHAT BUSINESS FOR YOU? . . .

Thumb through the yellow pages of your telephone directory. There are a thousand businesses you could go into. Which shall it be? Let's assume you don't have your mind made up in advance; you aren't set on the flower business because you love flowers or on starting a health-food store because you believe in natural foods. You're open to suggestion. Good! Your Uncle Sam is Johnny on the spot with the best, the most complete, the most reliable information you can hope to get anywhere. He will flood you with printed material all aimed directly at your own problems.

For an over-all survey of the whole situation, we turn first to the Small Business Administration's wonderful Starting and Managing Series. These authoritative government books deal with key aspects of starting and managing a specific kind of small business. Here is a rundown on the first eight books in this series.

1. *Starting and Managing a Small Business of Your Own.* Describes the common problems of launching small business operations in general, suggesting specific steps to help those interested in starting and managing a small business to arrive at sound decisions concerning these problems.

2. *Starting and Managing a Small Credit Bureau and Collection Service.* Supplies fundamental background information needed by those interested in starting and operating credit bureaus and collection services; provides assistance for those who are now active in the field, for the improvement and refinement of their operations.

3. *Starting and Managing a Service Station.* Provides information of value to both the newcomer and the veteran service-station operator. For the prospective dealer, it provides a guide to operating conditions in the field—one that spells out for them both common problems and pitfalls as well as potential rewards. For those already in business, it discusses the broad area of administration and long-range planning.

4. *Starting and Managing a Small Bookkeeping Service.* This booklet should have a special appeal to prospective owner-managers of a small bookkeeping service. It discusses what public bookkeeping is like; what it also takes to start a small bookkeeping service; what services to provide; where to locate; what you will earn; what sort of organization you need; and planning for the future.

5. *Starting and Managing a Small Business.* This volume is intended for prospective and newly established builders who are concerned primarily with

small repairs and modernization and with building homes, small business buildings, and the like, as well as with expansion and remodeling of existing small structures.

6. *Starting and Managing an Aviation Fixed Based Operation.* Describes the advantages and disadvantages of going into this particular business, the risks involved, the personal characteristics that will contribute to success. and some of the management practices whose application is necessary for the successful operation of that business.

7. *Starting and Managing a Small Motel.* This publication, prepared to supply new and inexperienced owner-managers with basic management knowhow, deals with the opportunities, risks, and problems involved in going into the motel business.

In addition to the above titles, you can also get the following books in this series:

Starting and Managing a Small Duplicating Service
Starting and Managing a Small Restaurant
Starting and Managing a Small Retail Hardware Store
Starting and Managing a Small Retail Drugstore
Starting and Managing a Small Drycleaning Business
Starting and Managing a Small Automatic Vending Business
Starting and Managing a Carwash

The titles in this list of the Starting and Managing Series range from 25 cents to 60 cents each. At random, let's look into one of these: *Starting and Managing a Small Building Business.*

For your 35 cents you get over 100 pages of solid know-how, condensed from a lifetime of experience by recognized experts in the field. Fourteen chapters take you through such problems as:

The final chapter directs you to sources for further information. This, incidentally, is standard with Government publications; they almost always wind up with a list of references to help you get still more knowledge about the subject under discussion.

I can personally cite a true example of how one of these books saved a friend of mine thousands of dollars. We were having lunch together one day, and he casually mentioned that he and his father were going to buy a motel the following day. I asked him what he knew about the motel business, and he replied, "Nothing at all, and neither does my father; but the place we're buying is a real gold mine! You should see the business they do each day!"

He went on to tell me that they had examined the owner's books, and he was ready to put his life savings and the life savings of his father into this new venture.

I persuaded him to go down to the offices of the Small Business Administration in Los Angeles and buy a copy of the book, *Starting and Managing a Small Motel*. He promised to buy the book and read it before he completed his negotiations on the purchase of the motel. Two days later he came into my office full of gratitude. He told me that this 30-cent book was responsible for saving him and his father their life savings. The book pointed out many facets of motel operation that he never suspected existed. It also told him what to look for when buying an established motel; and it was this particular information that opened his eyes to the poor investment he was ready to make.

But let's say that motels, service stations, or credit and collection are not your dish of tea. Will you have to wait until the SBA gets around to a booklet in this series on the business *you* are interested in? Not at all. The SBA puts out sixty-eight (as of today) *Small Business Bulletins*. They cover a large number of businesses as well as some general problems common to all businesses. More of these bulletins are coming out all the time. They're absolutely free. Whether your taste runs to retailing, service industry, manufacturing, you'll find unbiased, factual, down-to-earth *expert* advice. The government has no ax to grind, no supplies to sell you, no fear of hurting your feelings with the hard truth where it will save you money, time, and grief.

Let's examine a couple of these bulletins to see the kind of information you're getting. Many of them are just bibliographies, a few pages long, telling you where to go for your information. Others are more complete. For instance, SBB No. 3, *Selling by Mail Order*, explains mail order rather fully, tells about the market, the kinds of goods to choose and the kinds to stay away from; it tells about proper pricing and markup and sources for getting your merchandise. You're told how to get or build a mailing list, how to key advertisements so you'll know which publications are pulling orders and which are wasting your advertising money. More dope is given on rules and regulations you must know and follow: the postal rules, other federal laws; what to do about a firm name.

Then comes the list of government and other publications you can turn to for more information. This booklet, like all of the SBB series, costs you just a smile . . . no money!

Since mail order is my own business, I can vouch for the straight-from-the-shoulder, accurate information this SBB booklet contains. I have seen many commercial mail-order courses selling for as high as $100 that are far less illuminating than this free business booklet. If mail order is your cup of tea, another excellent Small Business Bulletin is No. 29, *National Mailing List Houses*. This is a directory of compilers or brokers of mailing lists of national scope. It tells you how to contact companies who deal in the business of renting names and addresses on different potential buyers for your products. To give you an idea of the diversity you'll find with the aid of this booklet, you can locate mailing lists of aviation manufacturing executives, elderly persons, farmers, fire chiefs, food brokers, hardware wholesalers, lawyers, mail-order buyers, ministers, newlyweds, opportunity seekers, single women, surgical-supply dealers, truck owners, veterans of the Korean conflict, wealthy persons, and wine distributors. How diversified can you get!

Two excellent SBB booklets are *Handcrafts and Home Products for Profit and Home Businesses*. Both of these booklets can be quite valuable to a person wishing to go into business for himself. *Handcrafts and Home Products for Profit* is directed to those people who have attained a degree of expertness in some craft or skill and would like to build a business based on it. Woodworking, textile arts, metal arts, small-animal raising, and cooking are among the many pursuits carried on around the home that sometimes become the nucleus for a successful business enterprise. While this publication does not provide thorough coverage of handcrafts and home products made for profit, it points out the main considerations in a successful business of this sort and furnishes a few references to literature on a number of different crafts.

The booklet on *Home Businesses* is directed to those people who have some spare time and are looking for a way to turn it to an interesting and profitable use. The principal emphasis in this booklet is on the marketing of a product or service rather than on the creation of a product, and it deals primarily with those businesses that are essentially a one-man enterprise where the proprietor is working for profit and not a salary or a wage.

In addition to the booklets just described, there are at least sixty-five more SBB booklets now in print, with additional ones being added from time to time. Here's a list of SBB booklets now in print.

SMALL BUSINESS BULLETINS

1. *Handcrafts and Home Products for Profit*
2. *Home Businesses*
3. *Selling by Mail-Order*
4. *New Product Development and Sale*
5. *Containers and Packaging*
7. *Advertising — Volume and Expenditures*
8. *Operating Costs and Ratios—Retail*
9. *Market Research Procedures*
10. *Retailing*
11. *Operating Costs and Ratios—Wholesale*
12. *Statistics and Maps for National Market Analysis*
13. *National Directories for Use in Marketing*
14. *The Nursery Business*
15. *Recording Systems— Store and Service Trade*
16. *Store Location*
17. *Restaurants and Other Eating Places*
18. *Basic Library Reference Sources*

19. *Bakery Products*
20. *Advertising—Retail Store*
21. *Variety Stores*
22. *Automatic Laundries*
23. *Training Retail Sales People*
24. *Food Stores (formerly Grocery, Meat, Produce)*
25. *Frozen Foods and Lockers*
26. *Gift and Art Shops*
27. *Shopping Centers*
28. *Retail Store Hours*
29. *National Mailing List Houses*
30. *Voluntary and Cooperative Chains*
31. *Retail Credit and Collections*
32. *Selling/Servicing Mechanical Refrigerators and Air Conditioners*
33. *Drug Stores*
34. *Distribution Cost Analysis*
35. *Hardware Retailing*
36. *Jewelry Retailing*
37. *Buying for Retail Stores*
38. *Toys*
39. *House-to-House Selling*
40. *Laundry and Dry Cleaning*
41. *Mobile Homes*
42. *Bookstore Operations*
43. *Plumbing and Heating Job Shop*
44. *Job Printing Shop*
45. *Men's and Boy's Clothing*
46. *Woodworking Shops*
47. *Soft Frozen Dessert Stands*
48. *Furniture Retailing*
49. *Warehousing*
50. *Apparel/Accessories for Women, Misses, Children*
51. *Trucking and Cartage*
52. *Store Arrangement and Display*
53. *Hobby Shop*
54. *Interior Decorating*
55. *Wholesaling*
56. *Training Commercial Salesmen*
57. *Selling/Servicing Appliances, Radio, TV*
58. *Small Office Automation*
59. *Consumer Credit*
60. *Painting and Decorating*
61. *Catering*
62. *Sporting Goods*
63. *Footwear*
64. *Photographic Dealers and Studios*
65. *Real Estate and Insurance*
66. *Motels*
67. *Manufacturer's Agent*
68. *Discount Retailing*

One of the most informative books published by the Small Business Administration is entitled *A Survey of Federal Government Publications of Interest to Small*

Business and its purpose is to provide, in a single volume, information about publications of interest to small-business owners. From the vast output of booklets, pamphlets, and leaflets published by the various government agencies, those most likely to be of assistance to the small-business sector are listed in this survey. Some are for sale at nominal prices by the Superintendent of Documents, and many others may be obtained at no cost from the issuing agencies. All are readily available to the small-business owner-manager.

Some of the material listed in this survey outlines the help available from federal agencies. Other publications explain, in nontechnical language, the laws which the agencies enforce. Still others present statistical data useful in marketing or specialized information pertinent to particular industries or trades. Small-business operators interested, for example, in obtaining a government contract, improving their management, or extending marketing operations abroad will find publications listed in this survey which will provide them with useful information. Prospective businessmen or students will also find helpful references on many subjects relating to small-business management and operation.

To give you an idea of the scope of this book, here are a few of the many listings you'll find in it.

Costs of Operating Nursing Homes and Related Facilities

Advertising for Profit and Prestige

A Directory of Foreign Advertising Agencies and Marketing Research Organizations for the United States International Business Community

Sales Promotion Pointers for Small Retailers

Alaska: Its Economy and Market Potential

Selling to AEC (U.S. Atomic Energy Commission)

Special Sources of Information on Isotopes

USAEC Patents Available for Licensing
What's Available in the Atomic Energy Literature
Available Leaflets on Fisheries
Basic Library Reference Sources for Business Use
Catalog of United States Foreign Trade Statistical
   Publications
Data Sources for Plant Location Analysis
Federal Trade Commission List of Publications
List of Available Publications of the United States
   Department of Agriculture
Mobile Homes
Selected List of Publications on Social Security
Small Business Administration Publications
Small Plant Turnover and Failure
General Information on Copyright
Directory of National Associations of Businessmen
Direct Methods of Selling in Foreign Markets
Facts About Small Business Financing
Helping the Banker Help You
The Market for Food in Public Schools
Restaurants and Other Eating Places
Retail Produce Manual
Selling to Navy Prime Contractors
Selling Business Pooling for Defense, Production,
   Research and Development
Small Business Specialists and Advisers by Organiza-
   tion and States

BUTCHER, BAKER, CANDLESTICK MAKER?

Already it's clear that you'd better not plunge into some business for yourself without hard thinking, planning, even soul searching. Even if you've had experience in some other business or as an employee of a firm, large or small, you might not be aware of a vital detail which could mean success or failure.

More than 1,000 new businesses are started in the United States each day, including more than 900 businesses transferred from one owner to another. But get this: 930 businesses are *discontinued* each day! Such a turnover in business ownership indicates a real need for information about the responsibilities of starting and managing a business.

When you consider that you have at your disposal, through the Small Business Administration, the talents and brains of some of the best business heads in the country, it is really a crime to start into any business endeavor without first taking advantage of the advice and help available to you. You're paying for these services with your taxes. Take advantage of them!

WHAT ABOUT THE MONEY? . . .

All right. You've decided you're the type to succeed. You have some idea of what business you want to engage in. Next question: Capital.

Uncle Sam is right there to help you. Next to the veteran, the home buyer, and the farmer, he loves the small businessman the best.

We've listed below a number of agencies set up primarily to help finance either a starting or a going business.

1. Small Business Investment Companies (SBIC)

Small business investment companies may make long-term loans to incorporated and unincorporated small businesses in order to provide funds needed for sound financing, growth, modernization and expansion. Long-term loans, as used herein, means loans with final maturities of not less than 5 years and not more than 20 years.

An SBIC's long-term loan must be of such sound value, or so secured, as reasonably to assure repayment. They may bear interest at rates agreed upon between the SBIC and the borrower. However, the rate of interest may not exceed the maximum rate permitted by local law; where no local limit is fixed, the interest rate charged must be within the rate limits set forth in the SBIC's proposal for a license.

2. G.I. Business Loans

If you're a veteran and haven't used up your whole "entitlement," the Veterans Administration may guarantee part of a loan you need to undertake or expand a legitimate business or even to pay off delinquent debts incurred in your venture.

3. Federal Reserve Bank Loans

Again, you must first apply to a bank, as these loans are available only if loans through private sources cannot be obtained on reasonable terms. The Federal Reserve Banks are located in Boston, New York City, Philadelphia, Cleveland, Richmond, Atlanta, Chicago, St. Louis, Minneapolis, Kansas City, Dallas, and San Francisco. And there are branches in twenty-four other cities.

4. Export-Import Bank of Washington

This agency aids in financing to facilitate foreign trade. Again, first apply through your local bank.

5. Miscellany

Loans for farmers are handled through the Department of Agriculture, and loans for veterans through the Veterans Administration.

6. The Small Business Administration

The SBA itself maintains offices of Loan Administration and Processing to lend money to start and carry on small business ventures. We'll talk more about this in the chapters to come.

Then there is money available under the Area Redevelopment Act to help you locate or expand in an area where employment is down. See Chapter III for more on this.

The congressional Declaration of Policy in the Small Business Act states: "The Government should aid, counsel, assist, and protect, insofar as is possible, the interests of small business concerns in order to preserve free competitive enterprise . . . and to maintain and strengthen the overall economy of the Nation."

With all the assistance the government is ready to give, you will have to admit that they are living up to their "Declaration of Policy."

BIBLIOGRAPHY

Department of Commerce Publications. 25 cents.
(Selected Publications Available from Local Department of Commerce Field Offices.)
Small Business Administration (Starting and Managing Series):
A Small Business of Your Own. 25 cents.
A Small Credit Bureau and Collection Service. 60 cents.
A Service Station. 35 cents.
A Small Bookkeeping Service. 30 cents.
A Small Building Business. 35 cents.
An Aviation Fixed Based Operation. 25 cents.
A Small Motel. 30 cents.

A Small Duplicating and Mailing Service. 25 cents.
Small business Bulletins (see above in this chapter for titles).
A Survey of Federal Government Publications of Interest to Small Business. 30 cents.

NOTE: To get these and all other publications we'll be mentioning in chapters to come:

(*a*) Go to the regional branch office of the department or agency which issues the publication; or

(*b*) Write to the main headquarters of the department or agency; or

(*c*) Write to the Superintendent of Documents, Washington, D.C. 20402; or

(*d*) Go to any of the 480-plus Depository Libraries to read the material. (Addresses of the libraries are listed in the *U.S. Department of Commerce Publications, 1963 Supplement.* 25 cents.)

Unless prices are given, the publications are free. If a charge is made, send money order or check with your order.

CHAPTER II

UNCLE SAM AS YOUR
BUSINESS ADVISER

RUNNING YOUR OWN BUSINESS
WITH GOVERNMENT HELP

UNCLE SAM IS "JOHNNY ON THE SPOT" . . .

Almost everyone in this country remembers the terrible disaster which took place in my city some time ago: the bursting of the Baldwin Hills dam in Los Angeles. Within twenty-four hours after that nightmare event, before the victims even had a chance to come out of their shock and give a thought to the crushing blow they had sustained in the destruction of several millions of dollars in property, the Small Business Administration had set up makeshift offices in nearby schools and were offering long-term 3 per cent government loans to businessmen whose shops and stores had been gutted and whose fixtures and stocks were destroyed by water, mud, and contamination.

This is a dramatic example of Uncle Sam's going beyond the call of duty to keep the businessman on an even keel, no matter what problems he may run into. Let's hope that *your* business is never hit by a flood or other disaster. Even without such extremes, you'll have problems enough. But Uncle is right there to help out with your little headaches as well as your big ones.

OFF AND RUNNING . . .

All right, enough of morbid thoughts. You're established in business; you've got your retail, wholesale, service, or manufacturing organization going. What can you expect from your beneficent Uncle Sam?

The answer is . . . plenty!

We've been talking about loans, money. The sources of loans listed in Chapter I are not earmarked for *starting* businesses alone. You're perfectly welcome to tap these agencies for money to get over the difficult first years, or to wait out a bad season, or to carry you through a period of poor-paying customers, or to help a business "even out" the rough spots, wherever they occur. If you have a business you believe in, in which you've invested your own time, sweat, and money, many times it's worth the added risk of borrowing to keep it going. So keep those agencies alive in the back of your mind. Maybe you won't need them, but it's mighty comforting to know that they're around if you do.

THE DEPARTMENT OF COMMERCE . . .

In the previous chapter we told you something of the help offered by the Department of Commerce for beginners in business. By its very nature, this department is geared to help business in every stage, and practically all the material we'll discuss in this chapter originates there. At the risk of repeating a few things, I believe it's worth pounding away at the work of this great agency.

In general, from Honolulu to Boston, from Miami to Seattle, the Field Offices of the United States Department of Commerce are "in business to aid business." Every business firm and organization is a welcome "client" at the Commerce Field Office in its locality. The basic job of each Field Office is to help make business better in its area and to aid local business firms in improving and expanding their operations. The Field Office brings the resources and services of the Commerce Department to your doorstep.

A Local Department of Commerce

In effect, each Field Office is a small-scale Department of Commerce in its own locality. The offices are usually located in business centers so that services of the U. S. Department of Commerce will be more immediately available to businessmen. Accordingly, letters to the Department in Washington are often referred to a Field Office, and a businessman who needs prompt service usually finds it advisable to consult his Field Office directly. The Field Office also gives out Census Bureau data and serves as a local information center for other Commerce agencies, including the National Bureau of Standards, U.S. Patent Office, U.S. Travel Service, and Area Redevelopment Administration. In addition, the Field Office advises and assists you in matters pertaining to the Agency for International Development (AID).
Bank, and the Foreign Credit Insurance Corporation (FCIC).

A Trained Staff of Business Specialists

At each Field Office, experienced business specialists will assist you in the solution of business problems, furnish information and publications on the programs and services of the Commerce Department and other federal agencies, and provide counsel on both foreign and domestic business operations. These trained staff members are also available to address business groups in the area.

A Wide Range of Business Publications

Each Field Office maintains an extensive business library of government and private reports, publications, periodicals, and directories. It also stocks and sells many useful publications on business subjects issued by the Superintendent of Documents for your convenience.

Domestic Trade

The Field Offices have a vital part in carrying out the Commerce Department's statutory responsibility to "foster, promote and develop the foreign and domestic commerce . . . of the United States."

To encourage and assist your domestic trade, each Field Office can furnish current, accurate, and dependable information on:

American Business and Industry—including material on production, output, sales, raw-materials sources, industry trends and prospects, marketing practices, location factors, and the operation of wholesale, retail, and service businesses.

American Science and Technology—including information on new discoveries and inventions, new products and processes, patent licensing, industrial standards, and the utilization of new technical knowledge and methods.

The American People—including facts on population, migration trends, housing, personal income, consumer markets, buying patterns, and employment.

The American Economy—including material on national income, the national product, national and regional economic trends, domestic markets and market potentials, balance of payments, foreign-aid programs, and business indexes, indicators, and forecasts.

Each Field Office Director and his staff of business specialists is anxious to help increase your domestic business activity in his area and to help local businesses expand and prosper.

At each Field Office, the facilities and services of the Commerce Department are free to all types of business firms, trade and professional associations, advertising agencies, communications media, local and state government agencies, and other persons and organizations interested in business matters.

Co-operative Offices in More than 500 Locations

To make the Commerce Department's facilities and services even more accessible to you, some 560 business organizations located in fifty states and Puerto Rico are serving their areas as "Co-operative Offices" of the United States Department of Commerce. Be sure to ask your Field Office where the nearest "Co-op" in your line is located.

These organizations include local and state Chambers of Commerce, manufacturers' associations, and state and municipal development commissions. Each maintains close liaison with the Field Office serving its area.

In these Co-operative Offices, many of the department's reports and publications are available for reference use. Business problems requiring counsel and assistance not available at a Co-operative Office will be referred to the nearest Field Office of the department.

AND THAT AIN'T ALL!

All this briefs only a part of what the Department does for the businessman. In a later chapter, for example, we'll take up the astounding variety of helps it offers the businessman who wants to expand into foreign trade through the department's Bureau of International Commerce.

But for the purposes of this chapter, we'll confine ourselves to another bureau we've already mentioned: the Small Business Administration.

Go back and look again at the list of *Small Business Bulletins*. In the last chapter we discussed them in terms of starting your business. Now that you glance over the list again, you'll see that a great many of them are slanted just as much toward helping you *run* your business, once it's under way. For example, take SBB (Small Business Bulletin) No. 7, *Advertising* or No. 9, *Market Research Procedures* or No. 11, *Operating Costs and Ratios—Wholesale*. Furthermore, throughout the series, tips and information useful in operating a going business are scattered like plums in a pudding. And, of course, the references—the books and publications which you're led to examine through the suggestions in the bulletins—will contain still more information on keeping your business head above water, once you've plunged into the drink!

However, all this is just the appetizer before the feast. The Small Business Administration publishes still more books or booklets which come right to the "meat and potatoes" for the operating businessman. The booklets are broken down into four major categories:

1. Management Aids
2. Technical Aids

3. Small Marketers Aids

4. Management Research Summaries

Altogether they add up to about 440 titles, and all are *free!*

Here are some of the more important of the titles in these four categories of booklets. Check off the numbers you're interested in.

Management Aids

17. *How the Walsh-Healey Public Contracts Act Affects Government Supply Contractors*

19. *Two Dozen Ideas for Effective Administration*

31. *Packaging Pointers for Government Contractors*

32. *How Trade Associations Help Small Business*

41. *How the Public Employment Service Helps Small Business*

42. *Getting Your Product on a Qualified Products List*

46. *How to Analyze Your Own Business*

49. *Know Your Patenting Procedures*

52. *Loan Sources in the Federal Government*

53. *Small Business Profits from Unpatentable Ideas*

75. *Protecting Your Records Against Disaster*

80. *Choosing the Legal Structure for Your Firm*

82. *Reducing the Risks in Product Development*

85. *Analyzing Your Cost of Marketing*

92. *Wishing Won't Get Profitable New Products*

105. *Watch Your Cash*

106. *Arbitration and the Small Businessman*

108. *Selecting a Lawyer for Your Business*

110. *Copyrights and Copyright Office Services*

112. *Responsibility Accounting Can Pay Dividends*

113. *"Tailor Make" Your Executive Staff*

114. *How the Commerce Department Helps Small Manufacturers in Foreign Trade*

Technical Aids

Small Marketers Aids

53. *Business Enterprises of Negroes in Tennessee*
54. *Investment Decision Making in Small Businesses*
55. *Small Business Development in New Hampshire*
56. *Use of Outside Information in Small Firms*
57. *A Study of SBA Financial Assistance in Utah*
58. *Small Business Success and Failure Cases*
59. *The Pine Lumber Industry in Mississippi*
60. *Small Business and Union-Wide Bargaining*
61. *A Study of Industry Financial and Operating Ratios*
62. *Maine's Potential for Wood Particle Board Manufacture*
63. *Small Business Problem Studies*
64. *Problems of South Carolina Food Processors*
65. *Mississippi's Forest Resources*
66. *Accounting in Small Business Decisions*
67. *Equity Financing of Small Manufacturing Firms*
68. *Sources of Equity and Long-Term Financing for Small Manufacturing Firms*
69. *Small Suppliers in a Changing Market*
70. *Advertising in Small Retail Stores*
71. *Export Trade and the Small Manufacturer*
72. *Insurance Management in Small Firms*
73. *Problems of Tennessee's Small Meatpackers*
74. *Employee Training Needs of Small Montana Firms*
75. *Small Business Patterns in Arizona*
76. *Accounting Practices in Small Firms*
77. *Small Lead-Zinc Mining in Montana*
78. *Site Evaluation for Small Retailers*
79. *Financing Small Manufacturing Firms in Maine*
80. *Small Business Use of Trade Association Programs*
81. *Business Methods in Small Personal Service Firms*
82. *Motor Freight Movements in Oklahoma*

Now, let's take a quick glance at a sample title from each series, to see what we're getting.

Management Aid No. 19 is entitled: *Two Dozen Ideas for Effective Administration.* Adapted from an article in *Modern Industry Magazine,* it gives you a capsule course on how to be a good manager: how to emphasize skill rather than rules in your organization, delegate responsibility, handle the problem of criticizing your workers without friction; how to get your staff to work actively and helpfully with your plans. All these and other tips can make the difference between a healthy, enthusiastic operation, with everybody working toward the same goals, and an "unhappy ship" with a Captain Bligh in charge, with the help determined not to give you a lick more work or brains than they have to.

Small Marketers Aid No. 21 discusses pricing and profits in small stores. It points out that there is no single success-producing formula in setting prices. It goes into detail on how to decide on markup, price lines, the one-price policy, and then offers some great suggestions on meeting price competition. The big answer, says the booklet, is doing things *better* than the other fellow. What things? Well, you can specialize with distinctive merchandise and private brands or you can work on personal salesmanship, seeing that your salespeople deal with customers as people—individuals—rather than treating them as an impersonal "public." It further points out that you can also buck lower-priced competition by:

1. Timing special sales to keep your stocks down and to take advantage of new merchandise on the market.

2. Watching trends, like do-it-yourself activities, hi-fi, stereo, and adapting your plans to feature them.

3. Emphasizing prestige . . . doing something the other fellow can't do . . . giving your store and advertising a "personality" of its own.

4. Offering extra services and conveniences, such as delivery, parking space, night openings, liberal policy on returns.

5. Remembering that a dollar saved in expense is worth ten in sales. Keep those expenses down, but not in ways that will show to the customer!

6. And finally, getting active in community relations. Be more than a businessman; become someone who is known for civic activities. You'll profit more if profit is *not* your only drive.

Technical Aid No. 28 tells you how to save plant expense through economies in lubrication. In a survey of over 900 companies using machinery, the net profits averaged 7 per cent of sales, while maintenance cost ran to 3 per cent of sales. If that 3 per cent could be cut in half through good maintenance and lubrication practices, the saving could be added to profit and the net profits would be boosted to 8½ per cent. In a plant selling $1,000,000 in goods a year, that increase means $15,000 in pure profit gravy!

The booklet then shows some case studies of money

saved through correct lubrication. Some plants reported a 30 per cent increase in production!

Another title in this series, *Essentials in Good Plant Lubrication*, Technical Aid No. 32, goes into the lubrication story from the other side, advising on selection of proper lubricants and outlining the responsibilities of the people doing this important job.

LIKE BANANAS, THEY COME IN BUNCHES ...

The Technical Aids, Marketers Aids, and Management Aids come bound in annual books, each containing a dozen or more of the most important titles. You can order these from the Superintendent of Documents as follows:

Management Aids for Small Business: Annual No. 1. 65 cents.

Management Aids for Small Business: Annual No. 2. 55 cents.

Management Aids for Small Business: Annual No. 3. 45 cents.

Management Aids for Small Manufacturers: Annual No. 4. 45 cents.

Management Aids for Small Manufacturers: Annual No. 5. 45 cents.

Management Aids for Small Manufacturers: Annual No. 6. 30 cents.

Technical Aids for Small Business: Annual No. 1. $1.00.

Technical Aids for Small Business: Annual No. 2. 50 cents.

Small Marketers Aids: Annual No. 1. 45 cents.

Small Marketers Aids: Annual No. 2. 40 cents.

In addition to these series—free if you order them as separate pamphlets—the SBA also puts out a Small Business Management Series. These are fuller, more detailed studies of management problems costing from 15 cents to 35 cents. Here are the twenty-three titles out so far (and don't forget that new ones are being added all the time).

Small Business Management Series

1. *An Employee System for the Small Plant.* 15 cents.
2. *One Hundred and Fifty Questions for a Prospective Manufacturer.* 20 cents.
3. *Human Relations in Small Industry.* 30 cents.
4. *Improving Materials Handling in Small Plants.* 20 cents.
5. *Public Accounting Services for Small Manufacturers.* 15 cents.
6. *Cutting Office Costs in Small Plants.* 25 cents.
7. *Better Communications in Small Business.* 20 cents.
8. *Making Your Sales Figures Talk.* 20 cents.
9. *Cost Accounting for Small Manufacturers.* 35 cents.
10. *Design Is Your Business.* 25 cents.
11. *Sales Training for the Small Manufacturer.* 20 cents.
12. *Executive Development in Small Business.* 25 cents.
13. *The Small Manufacturer and His Specialized Staff.* 20 cents.
14. *The Foreman in Small Industry.* 20 cents.
15. *A Handbook of Small Business Finance.* 30 cents.
16. *Health Maintenance for Greater Efficiency.* 25 cents.

17. *New Product Introduction for Small Business Owners.* 30 cents.
18. *Profitable Advertising for Small Industrial Goods Producers.* 35 cents.
19. *Technology and Your New Products.* 25 cents.
20. *Ratio Analysis for Small Business.* 25 cents.
21. *Profitable Small Plant Layout.* 25 cents.
22. *Practical Business Use of Government Statistics.* 20 cents.
23. *Research Relations Between Engineering Educational Institutions and Industrial Organizations.* 25 cents.
24. *Equity Capital and Small Business.* 35 cents.

These Small Business Management Series are not bibliographies or pamphlets, but books of 50 to 100 or more pages, covering all aspects and sides of the subject. Let's take a closer look at one of them.

Small Business Management Series No. 18 *Profitable Advertising for Small Industrial Goods Producers.* Suppose you're a small manufacturer of industrial goods—fabricated metal products for construction, let's say. Should you advertise? How much should you budget for advertising? How should you choose an agency? What will be the functions of your own advertising manager? Does advertising pay in a product like yours, anyway?

These and a thousand other questions you'd be asking yourself about advertising are answered here. Note first how the booklet doesn't attempt to cover *all* advertising situations. Even in the manufacturing field, it limits its range to industrial products. Advertising for consumers' products is covered in other places.

The booklet is divided into two sections: the first for owners and top executives, the second directed at advertising managers. Many problems are covered; we have time to skim over only a few. First of all, to the question, "Should I advertise?" the answer is a resounding "Yes!" The booklet states:

> What is your company's most important function? Obviously, most company functions are important. Before a product is manufactured, it must be conceived, engineered, and developed. Materials must be procured and an efficient and economical production system must be established. Cost accounting is a necessary adjunct to the process. But one thing is certain: *Goods when produced represent costs; it it is only when they are SOLD that they turn into income!* Therefore, the primary responsibility of the owners of every business is to *sell* the product. Companies often rise or fall upon successes or failures in sales.
>
> *Three Avenues of Selling.* That you may sell, you must TELL. You must get the *right story* to the *right people* in the *right way* at the *right time*. Three avenues exist over which you can broadcast your sales message—(1) through personal selling (by company salesmen), (2) by sales promotion (the inspiration of distributor and/or dealer sales activity in your behalf), and (3) by advertising (through impersonal salesmen such as trade magazines, newspapers, and direct mail).

Thus advertising is put in its proper place: along with your salesmen, as a sales tool you can't afford to do without any more than you'd cut out your sales staff.

The booklet goes on to help you set your advertisnig objectives and then proceeds to the organization problems: planning, and selecting your advertising manager and advertising agency.

I'd say that 99 out of 100 small businessmen wouldn't

know the first thing about how to select an agency. It's as risky as selecting a wife; but, fortunately, a few rules can be laid down about picking an agency! The book's very first word on the subject can save you endless grief: "Never select an agency for purely personal reasons. The fact that it's run by your brother-in-law doesn't make it the right agency for you. Matter of fact, that very relationship can make it the *wrong* one."

But you can check into the prospective agency's qualifications by asking what success they've had with other clients, nosing into their reputation (even among competitors), examining the training and experience of the people in the agency, getting a line on their creative abilities and imagination and what they know about markets, media, etc. How long have the present clients been with the agency? How many have they lost over the last few years?

After a grilling like this, you'll have a pretty good idea of what you're getting into. But the book doesn't stop with putting you into the agency's hands. It continues, educating you on sound advertising practices, covering newspaper, periodical, direct-mail, and other types; it tells you how to evaluate results, how to keep records, and gives many other pointers. It concludes with actual case histories and the usual list of solid books, magazines, and other places to get still more information. This could be the best thirty-five-cent investment you've ever made!

HOW TO READ AN ACCOUNT BOOK . . .

When Abe Lincoln ran his log-cabin general store, he figured that if he bought a cord of wood from a farmer for a dollar and sold it to a householder for two dollars, he made a dollar profit. Business *used* to be that simple; but no longer. Abe didn't have to pay rent for his store or the land it stood on, didn't advertise or count interest on his invested capital, didn't have a payroll, didn't figure in the value of his own time or the depreciation on his tools. His selling price on the wood—his "ratio" of sales to cost—was two to one.

Today, if you try to work on Abe's figures, you'll probably be operating at a *loss* because cost is only one of the many factors (some hidden) you have to take into account in setting your selling price to come out ahead. That's why, before leaving this absolutely diamond-studded series of *Small Business Management* pamphlets, I want to give you a bird's-eye view of just one more. This is No. 20, *Ratio Analysis for Small Business*. Ratio is not the easiest thing in the world to grasp, but it can mean the difference between business failure and success because, the author points out, most small-business failures are due to weaknesses in the *management* of the business. In spite of the advantages of small business—simplicity, adaptability, quick decision possibilities, and the like— the small-business manager has to wear many hats. Some fit him better than others.

Do you know how to figure in every expense and overhead item in setting *your* selling costs? What are your policies on credit—especially the borderline risk cases? How's your inventory control in relation to your sales and operating capital? Are you counting in assets like real estate, machinery, equipment, and fixtures when figuring your capital? How do you manage your current and long-term liabilities? Are you keeping future growth in mind and setting aside money to finance it?

If any of these questions cause you to scratch *your* head, this is a book for you to read. I don't go into the technical details; that's something for you to work out with your accountant. But a case history cited in the book may give you a graphic idea of some possible shortcomings of your own. I'll just quote part of it.

The banker motioned to his visitor. "Come in, Dave; sit down." When Dave was seated, Tompkins opened his desk drawer and pulled out a group of sheets containing columns of figures posted on comparative forms. The lumberman guessed that they were his.

"Glad you came in. I've been wanting to have a chat with you for quite a while." Then followed a moment of silence as the banker stared out the window. Finally, he continued: "Dave, you're a good salesman, and you know lumber. How well do you know your own figures?"

"I don't know, Mr. Tompkins. The bookkeeper gives me monthly statements—sales, cash, and expenses. She runs off a balance sheet once a year when we take inventory—taxes, you know, and all that. Most of the time, I'm too busy in the yard to go into the ledgers. I leave most of the details to her."

The banker waited and then went on. "Let me ask you another question, Dave. Why do you insist on doing business for nothing?" Dave was startled, and he began to flush. He had been expecting to be taken to task for the overdue note, and had thought himself reasonably well fortified with reasons. But the conversation was now taking a turn for which he was unprepared.

"I'm *not* working for nothing," Dave countered. "Last two years, it's been tough. I've been building up business—you know that. Look at my history. I'm worth more than . . ."

"Wait a minute, Dave. I know what you're going to say. But just look at your figures. Last year, you netted $1,700. The year before, it was $750, and that was before your taxes. You could have done better working for someone else. Lots of yards would have been glad to have you as a salesman or yard manager at your same salary and profit. You made virtually nothing on invested capital."

"But how much should I have made?" Dave asked.

"You know, Dave, the amount of profit a concern 'should earn' on its capital is something of an academic question. Some say that the ratio of net profits after taxes to tangible net worth should be between 5 and 10 percent. I look at it this way: If you'd gone to work for someone else, and invested your $64,000 in blue-chip securities, you could have safely earned around 5 percent in dividends. That's— let's see, nearly $3,100—almost twice your earnings before taxes.

"Anyway, let's be practical. Your net profit on net sales for the year was just under one-half of 1 percent. Your State Association of Lumber Dealers reports that its studies indicate an average return for its members of close to 3½ percent on sales—7 times what you're getting."

Dave was quiet. The point had been driven home. The banker softened. "Of course, Dave, when you missed receiving your 2 percent discount on some $300,000 in purchases, I know that it hurt."

"Sure," Dave came back, "but it takes money to take discounts. Why if I had more capital—say $40,000 more—it would be a cinch. But where would I lay my hands on that kind of cash?"

"Maybe, Dave, you've got all the capital you're going to need," said the banker, as he spread out the Middleville Lumber Co.'s figures over his desk. "You know, Dave, I'm convinced you have been violating three commandments of financial management."

"Now, wait a moment, Mr. Tompkins!" Dave

countered. "You know as well as I do, I'll never borrow a dime I can't pay back, nor buy a two-by-four I won't pay for. I'm solvent. Look at my figures. I've got assets to pay."

As Dave broke off, the banker picked up the figures and continued, "Don't get upset. I know you're honest, and I know your intentions. If we weren't sure about that, I wouldn't be talking to you. I'm thinking of something else. The three commandments I mentioned are something I heard a speaker refer to once. They are: Don't overbuy, don't overtrade, don't overexpand. Now don't you agree you've done all three?"

Dave hedged, "Well—what makes you think so?"

"Look here." The banker and the lumberman drew up their chairs. "Let's start with your balance sheet. You show current assets of $130,000 and current debts of $88,000. Your current ratio is 1.47 to 1. That's dangerously close according to your association. They've felt that the average lumberyard should show—at a minimum—a ratio of 3 to 1. Other studies I've seen indicate a prevailing median current ratio of 3.4 to 1. So to my eye you look low on current ratio.

"Now take your working capital—current assets less current debts. In your case, it's $42,000. That's the money you would have left over, if you were to suddenly pay off all debts by liquidating current assets. It's the protective cushion you need to have in carrying your receivables and inventory. Last year, your ratio of working capital to net sales was about nine times. Experience suggests to me that four times would have been about right. Take your turnover of tangible net worth; by that I mean the ratio of your $66,000 in tangible net worth to $363,000 in net sales. It was nearly five and one-half times for the year. My observation is that it should have been a little more than two and one-half times. I'm basing that comment on some 'standard' ratios I obtained for the comparison. That's why I say I think you've been overtrading."

"What does all this standard-ratio stuff mean?" Dave interjected. "That fast figure work was a little over my head."

"It's simple enough if you figure it out in logical order, Dave. Overtrading with finances is something like speeding in a car. At 30 miles an hour, a blowout is an inconvenience—but at 80 miles an hour?"

Tompkins paused to let the point sink in.

"Look, Dave—what if one of your big customers goes sour and you have to write some big receivables off as bad debts? What if prices take a quick tumble and your inventory declines in value? What if building should suddenly come to a halt in this area because of a strike? How about your own health—what if you were to be sick? Suppose creditors demand their own money?

"Suppose . . . " and the banker smiled, "Suppose, Dave, we called your loan."

Dave glanced up quickly. "Okay, Mr. Tompkins, I see the point. How about the loan?"

"Let's think some things through first, Dave. We'll get to the loan—and we don't intend to see you forced out of business. But let's understand this: a soundly operated business has the strength to sustain blowouts. You haven't."

And that's about all we need of that, I guess. For the rest of the story, read the book. But maybe the little sample I quoted will make you re-examine your own buying, borrowing, pricing policies. Are they based on sound principles? Or do you just throw darts at a board to pick out the figures? If you're a "Dave," you'd better

straighten up and fly right. As the friendly banker con-
cluded, Dave was a good businessman, all right; he was
just shy on certain knowledge he needed to make his
business solid, sound, and profitable.

The book you're holding in your hand tells you
how to get $50,000 worth of business advice from the
United States Government.

Well, maybe in the past couple of pages you've
already had your $50,000 worth. If so, the following
chapters are pure gravy for you!

BIBLIOGRAPHY

Small Business Administration. *Profitable Advertising
for Small Industrial Goods Producers.* (Small Business Management Series, No. 18.) 35 cents.

———*Ratio Analysis for Small Business.* (SBM Series,
No. 20, 2d ed.) 25 cents.

———*Small Marketers Aids, Annual No. 2.* 40 cents.

———*Technical Aids for Small Business, Annual No.
2.* 50 cents.

CHAPTER III

UNCLE SAM AS YOUR
SALES PROMOTION MAN

BUILDING YOUR BUSINESS
WITH GOVERNMENT HELP

Once you've decided on your business, once you've got it rolling on an even keel, you can't just sit back and relax. Far from it! You've got to grab that car and keep moving forward.

Or, to put it in another way, you must recognize the unwritten rule of business, particularly American business: Progress or die.

And unless you keep constantly on the lookout for new ideas, new sources, fresh products to fit into your line, new uses for old products, and new markets for products both old and new, you can take it from me . . . your business will strangle and die.

Uncle Sam has been anxious to set you up in business and to point you in the right direction. He's just as anxious to give you a push when you falter. In this chapter, let's look into the aids for increasing your profits against the many elements which are constantly chipping away at them. In other words, let's see what your government can do to help you stay afloat in today's highly competitive market.

SOME BASICS . . .

There was a time when you could mind your own store and let the world take care of itself. Those days are gone. Today's businessman cannot remain content with a knowledge merely of his own line, his own industry and market area.

Recognizing this, the government supplies you with information about national and international conditions and changes affecting all business in general, plus your own business in particular. These changing conditions are kept up to the minute through a listing of the Department of Commerce: *Publications for Use in Marketing and Distribution.*

This is one of your sources for getting hold of the information you need to help you run your business and increase profits. Naturally, a good deal of the material will not pertain to your specific enterprise, but it's unlikely that you could thumb through an issue and not come upon something you can use. And remember, one little idea can be worth thousands of dollars.

Let's examine a typical copy of this basic information source. It opens with Census and General Business Statistics, offering about a dozen entries, already published or to be published shortly, in the areas of agriculture, business, governments, housing, manufactures, minerals, population.

Other sections cover domestic trade, foreign trade, etc., and tell you about the latest publications in these fields, what they cost, and where you can get them.

A sampling of a few of these entries gives some idea of the value you can expect from this periodical.

Location of Manufacturing Plants by Industry, County, and Employment Size. Series MC58(S)-2.1 to MC58(S)-2.9. Published in nine parts, ranging in price from 40 cents to $1.00. Number of manufacturing plants classified by industry, state, county, and employment-size class.

Puerto Rico Census of Manufactures, MC-PR. Available free from Puerto Rico Planning Board, San Juan, P.R. Final summary statistics of manufacturing activity by industry and geographic area on such topics as value added by manufacture, employment, payrolls, inventories, and capital expenditures.

Statistical Abstract of the United States. Annual. $3.50. CS.134:961. The one-volume basic reference source is standard summary of statistics on social, political, and economic organization of the United States. Includes comprehensive selection of data from most important statistical publications, both governmental and private, and an extensive bibliography of statistical sources. Contains over 1,200 tables and charts.

Canned Food Report. Series Bi. Issued five times a year. Subscription, 50 cents for one season; 10 cents a copy. Bureau of the Census. Data on stocks of wholesale distributors, canners, and warehouses of retail food chains. Coverage is for canned food items (vegetables, fruits, juices, and fish).

Travel Survey. 25 cents. Bureau of the Census. Presents data on overnight trips or one-day trips to a place at least 100 miles (one way) from traveler's home. Detail tables on number of trips and trip days in business travel, personal trips to visit friends and relatives, vacation trips, and other travel. Shows means of transportation, distance to major destinations, income level of traveler, and other factors.

Alaska: Its Economy and Market Potential. 61

pp., 70 cents. C41.2:AL IS. Review of major economic aspects of new state, including appraisal of business and employment prospects. Chapters devoted to: land and people; market characteristics; natural resources and their development, tomorrow's challenge.

Handbook of Federal Aids to Communities. 69 pp., 45 cents. C46.8:C73. Listing of government services and resources that may be helpful to communities seeking to develop or improve their economic status and to diversify or expand their economies. Outlines more than a hundred types of community assistance offered by federal agencies and indicates where complete information may be obtained.

General Information Concerning Patents. 39 pp., 15 cents. C21.2:P27/960. Contains general information about trade-marks and Patent Office. (See also C21.2:T67/960.)

Official Gazette of the Patent Office. Weekly. 300–400 pp. Subscription, $30.00 per year, C21.5; 75 cents per copy. Lists the patents, trade-marks, and design patents issued each week, and decisions of Commissioner of Patents and of United States courts in patent cases. Last weekly issue of each month includes a section entitled "Bulletin of Decisions of Patent Office on Trademarks."

Patent Attorneys and Agents Available to Represent Inventors Before the U.S. Patent Office. 45 cents. C21.9/2:960. Geographical listings of individuals, with address.

Patents and Inventions. 25 pp., 15 cents. C21.2:P27/10. Explains importance of patents and summarizes six basic steps necessary to procure a patent. Discusses marketing and developing an invention.

Questions and Answers About Patents. 4 pp., free. Department of Commerce. Brief answers to twenty-eight questions about patents.

Questions and Answers About Patents. 4 pp.,
free. Department of Commerce. Brief answers to
twenty-six common questions about trade-marks.
Daily Weather Map. $9.60 per year. C30.12.
Consists of five maps, data for which are taken at
different hours at hundreds of stations throughout
North America. Includes data on temperature, pre-
cipitation, barometric pressure, and cloud type.
Business Service Checklist. Weekly. 4 pp. Subscription, $1.50 per year, C1.24; five cents a copy.
Lists all materials published each week by U.S. Department of Commerce and selected publications of
other agencies. News releases, books, pamphlets, reports, and other materials of interest to industry and
business.
Developing and Selling New Products. 105 pp.,
45 cents. C41.22:P94. Guidebook for manufacturers.
Describes steps that may be taken to meet problems
arising in planning new-product development and
marketing programs. Discusses such topics as locating
ideas for new products, improving chances for selection of successful new products, building products
to suit customer needs and desires, choosing name of
trade-mark, packaging, and planning marketing campaign. Gives new-product marketing case studies.
Points out government additional aids to new-product
development and marketing.
Marketing Information Guide. Monthly. Subscription (including supplements), $2 per year; 15
cents a copy; supplements, 20 cents each. C41.11.
Each issue contains about 150 annotations of selected
current publications and reports (both government
and nongovernment) with basic information and statistics on marketing and distribution. Government
periodical supplement in March; semiannual subject-
index supplements issued in January and July.
Directory of National Associations of Business-

men. 81 pp., 50 cents. C41.22:AS 7/961. Presents data on some 2,000 national organizations.

HOW TO REACH THE JAPANESE . . .

Possibly none of the subjects above is of interest to you. But you can be sure that ten minutes a month spent scanning the contents will turn up at least one lead that will spell dollars in your till. Let me give you a personal example.

I had a little item I felt would be good for the Japanese market. My problem was: how to reach the Japanese businessman? Advertise in the Tokyo papers? Which papers? What about the language barrier? I was mulling over the real problems and had just about given up the idea when an item in *Publications for Marketing* caught my eye. It led me to send for another publication, a *Directory of Foreign Organizations for Trade and Investment Promotion,* put out by the Bureau of International Commerce. We'll discuss the booklet more in detail in Chapter IV. For present purposes, I learned that every industry in Japan has an "association," and every association puts out regular bulletins to its members, advising them of trade opportunities. There is no charge for getting your product described in these bulletins, provided it is of real or possible use to the Japanese businessmen who subscribe.

Now get this. *There are over sixty* of these associations in Japan. They cover every industry from silks to pharmaceuticals, from pearls to bicycles. In addition, there are Chamber of Commerce bulletins in the various cities listing many "trade opportunities." So, for the price of a mimeographed letter and sixty air-mail stamps, I got my story before *five thousand* separate companies! I covered

my expenses with the first order, and there were plenty
more orders following the first.

STATISTICS ARE DOLLAR BILLS . . .

You're a functioning businessman, alert and eagerly
perceptive to the ever-changing world we live in . . . and
statistics are money in your pocket! If you don't believe
me, take a look at Small Business Management Series
Booklet No. 22, *Practical Business Use of Government
Statistics* (20 cents, as listed in Chapter II). This is a
brief, simplified introduction to a subject most people—
quite wrongly—shy away from. It's a good starting point
for newcomers to the field and a quick refresher for
others.

It points out that your Uncle Sam is the world's
largest producer of statistics. You've heard of the five-
foot shelf? Well, a file of all government statistics would
require literally *miles* of shelf space! Obviously, no one
person needs or could use even a fraction of them. So,
to help you find your way through this maze and to
ferret out the figures, trends, and forecasts which will
be meaningful to you, the Department of Commerce
publishes several summaries. And as a guide to the summaries, this little SBM No. 22 is very useful. It brings
the statistics down to earth, as it were, by relating them
directly to the businessman's problems, as can be seen
from the contents:

> *Markets*
> > How Big Is the Market?
> > Where Is the Market?
> > How to Sell to the Market
> > Industrial Markets

Competition and Product Information
   Company Results Compared with Industry
   Information on Raw Materials
   Data on Labor
   Business Indexes
How to Read Statistics
   How Good Are the Figures?
   What Do the Figures Really Mean?
Where To Find the Data
   Reference Sources
   Selected Government Statistics

Giving actual pages taken from various statistical publications, the booklet shows you how to read statistics, how to understand them, and how to apply them to your own uses. It gives actual examples and illustrations, for most types of businesses, of the use of different sources of statistics. The booklet winds up with a short discussion on how to read statistics, how to assess the accuracy of the figures, and how to interpret them. My guess is, after spending a half-hour with this 20-cent booklet, you'll never again look on statistics as dry stuff completely foreign to your business world.

Before leaving the subject of statistics, let me tell you about three excellent publications on this subject.

Statistical Abstract of the United States. This book covers a wide variety of subjects and contains over 1,100 tables. The *Abstract* is published yearly as a hard-cover, standard-size book and is sold for $3.50 by the Superintendent of Documents, Washington, D.C. 20402. In addition to selected statistics, the *Abstract* has a reference section for other sources of information. Because of its wide coverage, low price, and convenient size, the *Abstract* is the most useful single publication of government statistics.

County and City Data Book. For more local, geographic detail, the Department of Commerce publishes this volume. It presents a selection of available statistics for all counties and for cities of over 25,000 population. Priced at $5.25, it is published about once every three years and sold through the Superintendent of Documents, Washington, D.C. 20402.

Survey of Current Business. Monthly and quarterly statistics on a wide variety of subjects, but with no geographic detail, are published in this periodical. The yearly subscription is $4.00 for twelve issues, also from the Superintendent of Documents, Washington, D.C. 20402. In addition to varied and detailed information on income, production, prices, wages, employment, finance, foreign trade, and major industry groups (most of the data being shown month by month for the preceding year), each issue features articles on economic trends or other business subjects.

THE MEAT AND POTATOES . . .

Getting down to the meat of sales promotion, you could travel far and find less help than what's available in another Department of Commerce magazine, the *Marketing Information Guide.* The price of this excellent monthly magazine is $2.00 per year, or 20 cents per copy.

As the title indicates, this periodical channels and summarizes market information in the form of brief descriptive paragraphs. The terse, fact-packed style is shown by these few excerpts from a single issue.

(23.4) *Travel Information Offices Maintained by States and Territories in the United States.* (Infor-

mation Sources on International Travel, No. 2.) U.S.
Dept. of Commerce, Washington 25, D.C. 4 pp. 10
cents. Alphabetical listing by States and territories
of travel information offices which promote travel
to their individual areas.

(23.5) *The Automatic Vending Machine Industry: Its Growth and Development.* U.S. Dept. of
Commerce, BDSA. GPO. 22 pp. 15 cents. Examines
the prospects of automatic vending machine manufacturers and route operations, and provides basic
statistics and background data. For manufacturing
gives the nature of the industry, geographical distribution, mergers and specializations, manufacturing
processes, and impact of in-plant feeding; route operations description and trends. International trade for
vending machines discussed.

(23.6) *Mining Machinery and Equipment: Shipments and Related Data.* U.S. Dept. of Commerce,
BDSA. GPO. 4 pp. 5 cents. Presents six statistical
tables and brief analysis on the mining machinery
equipment industry for years 1955–61. Data summar-
ized by product code on number of producers, by
value of shipment, controlled material consumed,
number of plants and origin of shipments by State.

These are government publications. However, the
Guide is just as helpful with the works issued by private
publishing houses; for example:

(23.83) *Accounting Systems for Management
Control.* Francis E. Moore and Howard F. Stettler.
(Richard D. Irwin, Inc., 1818 Ridge Rd., Home-
wood, Ill.) 708 pp. $12.65. Discusses management in-
formation and control demands on the accounting
system. Considers the basic elements of the accounting system and explains how these systems are de-

veloped in relationship to the various operating functions of business. Also covers professional aspects of accounting systems work—the design and installation of systems. Includes questions, problems, and cases.

(23.84) *Advertising Art International.* (Modern Publicity Yearbook Number 32.) Hastings House, Publishers, 151 E. 50th St., New York 22, N.Y. Approx. 200 pp., 8½ x 11. $11.50. Reproductions (in black and white and color) of selected drawings and photographs used in advertising in U.S. and principal foreign countries. In each case indicates country, and media (or sub-class) in which illustration appeared. Introductory section discusses trends in modern advertising.

(23.85) *Guide to the Use of the Mails.* Henry A. Berg. Crane Press, Inc., 430 W. 16th St., New York 11, N.Y. 49 pp. $2.00. Compact handbook of postal data to those who employ the mails in conducting business. Sections on classes of mail and types of postal service. Pinpoints specific regulations, as limited mailable and unmailable items, and postal meter machines. Well illustrated with drawings. Detailed index of contents.

(23.86) *Industrial Purchasing: Principles and Practices.* Raymond R. Colton. Charles E. Merrill Books, Inc., 1300 Alum Creek Dr., Columbus 16, Ohio. 525 pp. $10.60. Provides fundamental information regarding procurement principles, procedures, and tools. Introduces established principles of purchasing and relates these principles to the specialized functions that have resulted from technological developments in the areas of materials, supplies, equipment, and services. In addition, gives attention to the specialized functions of scrap and waste recovery, expediting, scientific storage, value analysis, research, materials management, and traffic management.

The *Guide* also provides thumbnail accounts of what you can expect from various publications of state and local Chambers of Commerce, university press publications, and any other source material likely to be useful to the man trying to market his products. A special feature of one particular issue is a complete rundown on college and university magazines for use in marketing and economic research. Subscriptions to many of these are free, and others cost a few cents each. Here are a few entries to give you an idea of this seldom-tapped mine of valuable know-how.

> *Boston University Monthly Index of Business Activity: New England and United States.* Monthly. College of Business Administration, Boston University, Boston 15, Mass. 4 pp. Free.
>
> *Kansas Business Review.* Monthly. Center for Research in Business, The University of Kansas, Lawrence, Kans. 16 pp. Free.
>
> *Mississippi's Business.* Bimonthly. Bureau of Business and Economic Research, University of Mississippi, University, Miss. 6-8 pp. Free.
>
> *(Houston) The Business Review.* Monthly. Center for Research in Business and Economics, University of Houston, Houston, Tex. 16 pp. $3 per year; 25 cents per single issue.
>
> *(Michigan) Business Topics.* Quarterly. Bureau of Business and Economic Research, Graduate School of Business Administration, Michigan State University, East Lansing, Mich. 80 pp. On request to those concerned with business and economic matters.

Take another look at that offer from Michigan. *Eighty* pages of business reports, and absolutely free!

INTERESTED IN THE FOOD BUSINESS?

You can get dozens of merchandising aids that have been researched by the Agricultural Marketing Division of the U.S. Department of Agriculture. These reports are available from the Superintendent of Documents, Government Printing Office, Washington, D.C. 20402. Here are just a few of them. (Free unless price is given.)

Wholesaling

MRR-94   *Methods of Increasing Productivity in Modern Grocery Warehouses.* 25 cents.

MRR-142   *Methods of Increasing Labor Productivity in Multistory and Small One-Floor Grocery Warehouses.* 25 cents.

MRR-266   *The Use of Fieldmen by Wholesale Food Distributors and Affiliated Retailers.* 25 cents.

MRR-271   *Improved Methods Among Wholesale Food Distributors for Inventory Control, Sales Accounting, and Shipment of Merchandise.* Supp. 5 cents. 40 cents.

MRR-335   *Policies and Practices of Some Leading Institutional Wholesale Grocers.* 25 cents.

MRR-348   *Grocery Warehouse Layout and Equipment for Maximum Productivity.* 40 cents.

MRR-399   *Measures of Operating Efficiency in Wholesale Food Warehouse.*

MRR-411   *Cost Control in Retail Food Stores by Use of Wholesalers' Accounting Services.*

MRR-454   *Improved Accounting Methods for Wholesale Food Distributors.*

MRR-473   *Handling Groceries from Warehouse to Retail Store Shelves.*

MRR-502   *Evaluating Delivery Operations of Whole-sale Food Distributors.*

MRR-571   *Services of Institutional Wholesale Groceries—Opinions of Food Service Operators.* 45 cents.

Retailing

AIB-31   *The Check-Out Operation in Self-Service Retail Food Stores.* 40 cents.

MRR-7   *Some Improved Methods of Handling Groceries in Self-Service Retail Food Stores.* 55 cents.

MRR-30   *Better Utilization of Selling Space in Food Stores—Part I. Relation of Size of Shelf Display to Sales of Canned Fruits and Vegetables.* 20 cents.

MRR-41   *Receiving, Blocking, and Cutting Meats in Retail Food Stores.* 40 cents.

MRR-44   *Packaging and Displaying Meats in Self-Service Meat Markets.* 50 cents.

MRR-77   *Principles of Layout for Self-Service Meat Departments.* 25 cents.

MRR-104   *Improved Handling of Frozen Foods in Retail Stores.* 20 cents.

MRR-129   *Unloading and Receiving Produce in Retail Food Stores.* 20 cents.

MRR-137   *Survey of Distribution Practices for Prepackaged Frozen Meat.* 20 cents.

MRR-192   *Improved Methods of Trimming Produce in Retail Food Stores.* 35 cents.

MRR-278   *Packaging and Price Marking Produce in Retail Food Stores.* 50 cents.

MRR-501   *Display Location and Customer Service in Retail Produce Departments.*

MRR-551   *Improved Methods of Displaying and Handling Produce in Retail Food Stores.*

MRR-590   *Principles of Layout for Retail Produce Operations.* 35 cents.

MRR-628   *Centralized Fresh Meat Processing for Retail Food Stores—an Interim Report.*

AMS-237   *Control of Inventories in Retail Food Stores Through Use of Order Books.*

Retail Produce Manual

MB-2   *Organization of the Work Area for Handling Produce in Retail Stores.* 15 cents.

MB-3   *Ordering, Receiving, and Storage of Produce in Retail Stores.* 5 cents.

MB-4   *Trimming Produce in Retail Stores.* 25 cents.

MB-11   *Managing and Scheduling of a Retail Produce Department.* 20 cents.

MB-14   *Packaging and Price-Marking Produce in Retail Stores.* 25 cents.

A KIT OF MARKETING TOOLS . . .

The Department of Commerce puts out a series of free booklets under the general heading of *Promoting Economic Growth.* Three especially geared to marketing and sales promotion are:

1. *Find Your Market*
2. *Measure How's Business*
3. *Share in Area Growth*

The last of these tells the story of the Area Redevelopment Act, which helps business to expand or to establish in an area of poor employment. Naturally, Uncle Sam is primarily interested in wiping out the blight of unemployment and promoting the welfare of citizens everywhere. He feels, rightly, that one way to accomplish this is through more and bigger markets for *your* business. And here is the kind of aid the ARA is offering the businessman.

> The Area Redevelopment Act made available a specific kit of tools to help business establish or expand in areas of chronic unemployment or underemployment:
>
> 1. Low-interest, long-term loans for new or expanding business firms.
> 2. Loans and grants to communities to help provide public facilities needed if new firms are to be established or existing firms expanded.
> 3. Technical assistance to help break barriers to economic growth.
> 4. Programs to help train jobless workers in new skills required by an ever-changing industrial economy.
>
> To these basic tools, the Area Redevelopment Administration has added a variety of other services to business and industry, including:
>
> 1. Information on redevelopment areas, labor force and plant sites.
> 2. Studies of transportation, markets and sales.
> 3. One-stop service for businessmen seeking information on the programs of other federal departments and agencies that will help in their expansion plans in redevelopment areas.

The booklet goes on to explain the terms under which you can get a 4 per cent loan for business expansion and continues with a description of other services, such as man-power training programs (how to lower your company's "start-up" cost), information on plant sites, market analyses, transportation studies, and guidance in sales and marketing.

Find Your Market helps you to use federal census facts to aid your marketing. Study the material intelligently, and you'll be amazed at the opportunities to save money. Rather than costly experimentation, you'll get a bird's-eye view of your potential market in advance, helping you to lay out sensible territories for salesmen and to analyze their sales performance. You'll avoid expensive mistakes in locating plants, warehouses, and stores in the wrong places. Just a few examples show the practical uses of such reports for the businessman.

- A manufacturer who made a product for dairy farms used the census of agriculture to locate the counties with large numbers of dairy farms. He used the business census to see what kind of stores were in those areas to sell his products. When he sent salesmen out, he expected those who worked in the more prosperous areas to get more orders.
- In one instance, a businessman had an opportunity to invest in the manufacture of one-man haybalers. To determine the potential market, he obtained a special county-by-county tabulation of farms producing hay in quantity to justify purchase of such haybalers and then made his decision in favor of the investment. And, it proved to be a highly profitable operation; the census facts he needed to enter the undertaking cost him only a few hundred dollars.
- A recent case illustrates another use of Census Bureau statistics in making a business decision. A large oil company was building a new refinery and considered building a plant that would make chemical fertilizer from a by-product of the refinery. The fertilizer plant would be profitable only if the company could sell its product nearby. The company determined the size of this potential market by examining

such statistics as the size and number of farms in adjoining counties, the acreage in cropland, and the farm income.

• A department store which planned a suburban branch studied the suburban area carefully before it invested money. It found out how many other stores were in the area and how much business they did. It examined the population statistics to determine how many people lived there and whether another retail outlet was justified. Finally, it studied the people— particularly their incomes and personal characteristics —to decide what kinds of merchandise could be sold.

FOR THE MANUFACTURER . . .

The Management Aids series we mentioned previously devotes its issue No. 4 to the problems of the small manufacturer. It tells you how to broaden your operations, how to plan your working-capital needs, how to design and redesign products so as to make them salable. It also tells you how to use your banker's services, how to mechanize your office records, and even how to appeal in income-tax disputes! Each chapter is by a recognized expert in his field.

This book also takes you step by step through the process of redesigning your product, from your first looking-over to the actual job. It tells you what design is for and advises you about the all-important matter of appearance. The book ends with a word on the importance of actual packaging from the point of view of selling. As usual, a short list of sources for further reading is given. And this book of 78 pages costs you all of 45 cents!

My Cost 45 cents! My profit $25,000!

Take a look at the 105-page booklet published by the Department of Commerce: *Developing and Selling New Products*. To help reduce your risk in this area, it answers such questions as:

1. How and where can I find ideas for new products?
2. How can my company improve its chances of selecting a successful new product?
3. How can I build a new product suitable to customer needs and desires?
4. How should name, package, and trade-mark be chosen?
5. What points should I consider in planning a marketing program for a new product?

Tips to help you reduce product failures "to almost zero": what are they worth to you? The SBA asks only 45 cents!

I credit this 45-cent book with a personal profit of $25,000. How? Someone had offered us a rather interesting gadget. It consisted of a plastic case about the size of this book, in which a spool of paper could be rolled backward and forward, something like the film in a camera. As the paper was exposed under a clear window, you could read the information on the scroll, a bit at a time.

As I originally saw it, the spool gave a series of drink recipes. I wasn't enchanted with the bartending aspect, feeling that it had a limited market. Furthermore, the experience of the patent holder hadn't been too promising. But I felt that this basic idea was a good one. Fresh from reading *Developing and Selling New Products*, I set out to apply its principles toward making this little device salable. (Just to show that no one is perfect, I must admit that I considered teaching information, such as word spelling, simple arithmetic, and historical facts for little tots, and then discarded the idea. Five years later, teaching machines burst on the market full-bloom and are, at this writing, a hot mail-order item!)

Convinced that if I filed my problem in the back of my head, the answer would come sooner or later, I bided my time and kept my eyes open. When the lightning struck, it was in a peculiar way. I was in a drugstore, fingering through a little booklet on first aid. Before my mind's eye flashed page 30 of *Developing and Selling* in which a paragraph on Designing the Product was followed by a case study of a drug firm's experience. I suddenly realized the type of information that would go best on my roller: first aid! Johnny cuts a finger, develops a fever, or falls off his bike. You want to know what to do, and you want to know fast. Zip through the little scroll for the answer! So I turned the product into an automated first-aid box called "Dial-Aid," took it to a large drug chain, and walked out with a clean, quick sale of the whole package, on an exclusive basis!

And talking about redesigning. . . . In *How I Made $1,000,000 in Mail Order*, I devoted a whole chapter to the ways in which we find our products. A section of that chapter counsels you to use the Government Publication Services. In a sense, this entire book is an outgrowth of that section, because, of course, I could only hit the highlights then. So you might say that this book, itself, is a case study of a product redesign!

HOW TO PUT YOUR SALESMEN WHERE THE MONEY IS . . .

Take a look at another booklet put out by the Office of Domestic Commerce. It's called *How Manufacturers Reduce Their Distribution Costs*. Here, for 45 cents, you get 150 pages of absolutely invaluable information of the kind that can make or break your business.

Taking the experiences of actual companies on the firing line, the book shows you how they cut their selling costs. You can follow their step-by-step planning and operation.

Once you've grasped the concept of profitable and unprofitable customers, it's easy for you to analyze your own customer list in this light and to cut out expensive selling cost wasted on those who don't bring you the profit to justify it.

And there are plenty more tips in this one pamphlet. How are your products sold? Through route sales, direct shipments, sales through wholesalers? You're shown how to analyze them for profit—again with illuminating examples from the files of actual firms. Orders, territories, salesmen's effort, routing, cost analysis, products, and physical distribution are carefully considered.

As a final example of Uncle Sam's continuing interest in your business welfare, let me point to SBA's Management Series No. 15, *A Handbook of Small Business Finance*. The Foreword explains the purpose and scope of this highly popular 80-page pamphlet, which is yours for 30 cents. We quote:

> The objective of *A Handbook of Small Business Finance* is not to cover all phases of the subject. Nor is it to provide an exhaustive treatment of any one

topic. Rather, it is to furnish new owners and inexperienced managers with basic information to help them understand better the financial operations of their businesses. As such, this booklet should aid businessmen in making better use of the financial assistance available to them—and particularly from local banks—guiding them in measuring the progress of their operations.

Financial statements, management, banking relationships, term loans, accounts receivable, and inventory financing are covered in the text. Chapter VI outlines some of the sources for financial assistance, through private venture capital organizations and industrial foundations. The SBA's own lending and investment programs are also discussed.

I have to remind you again, at the risk of repeating myself, that my effort here is *not* to cover the entire subject of help from the government. It would be impossible—physically impossible—to take a complete tour of Uncle Sam's five-mile bookshelf. But if I can give you an inkling of what's on that shelf, where to go for more—if I can impart some of my own enthusiasm and pride in this government that thinks enough of its citizens to go to this tremendous labor in their behalf—I'll have accomplished what I set out to do. All I can do is point to where the pay dirt is. All you have to do is grab a shovel and dig!

BIBLIOGRAPHY

Small Business Administration. *Practical Business Use of Government Statistics.* (SBA Management Series, No. 22.) 20 cents.
———. *A Handbook of Small Business Finance.*

(Small Business Management Series, No. 15.) 30 cents.

————. *Developing and Selling New Products.* 45 cents.

Management Aids for Small Manufacturers, Annual No. 4. 45 cents.

U.S. Department of Commerce, Area Redevelopment Administration, Bureau of the Census. *Share in Area Growth.*

————. *Find Your Market.*

U.S. Department of Commerce, Office of Domestic Commerce. *How Manufacturers Reduce Their Distribution Costs.* 45 cents.

U.S. Department of Commerce. *Marketing Information Guide.* 15 cents.

————. *Publications for Use in Marketing and Distribution.* 20 cents.

CHAPTER IV

UNCLE SAM AS YOUR OVERSEAS ASSISTANT

The World—Your Oyster— with Government Help

Be glad you're doing business today instead of in the days before World War I. That war marked the end of an era for the United States, a period during which we distrusted and discouraged foreign trade. Later, the high tariff walls came tumbling down, and we learned that the world outside our borders was a great big market, hungry for goods with the "Made in U.S.A." stamp and ready to pay good prices for them.

To see how startlingly different things are today, all you have to do is glance through a slim blue leaflet put out by the Field Services of the Bureau of International Commerce, entitled *Services Available to U.S. Exporters.** It's a real eye-opener. Just listen:

> *Let Your Field Office Help You Research Foreign Markets.* Market research probably is even more important in foreign selling than in domestic. Trained business analysts in the Department's Field Offices

* The Bureau of International Commerce was formerly called the Bureau of Foreign Commerce, which accounts for the titles on some older publications. However, your inquiry to either will reach the Bureau.

will assist you in making a market analysis. With the aid of their extensive files and new data received daily, they will:

Help you determine which foreign countries are the best customers for your firm's products . . .

Tell you about the foreign country's import tariffs and import and exchange controls as they apply to your products . . .

Lend you copies of detailed descriptions of market conditions in the country of interest . . .

Furnish detailed current information on economic conditions in the country of interest . . .

Arrange for you to consult with Bureau of Foreign Commerce country specialists in Washington, if necessary. These specialists are highly trained international economists who concentrate on one or two countries and can answer most of your questions quickly and completely.

How the B.F.C. Helps You to Contact Foreign Firms Interested in Buying Your Products. The periodical *International Commerce* regularly carries reports of specific foreign businessmen who have visited our Embassies and Consulates to ask about buying specific U.S. products.

Trade lists, compiled by Commercial Officers in U.S. Foreign Service posts, list all reliable, significant foreign firms which import a specific commodity. Trade lists may be purchased from Field Offices or BFC for $2.00 each.

Trade Contact Surveys are quick, efficient methods of finding reliable and aggressive sales agents and distributors in foreign countries. At your request, experienced Foreign Service officers canvass particular foreign cities and report at least three companies which meet your requirements.

World Trade Directory Reports are valuable and they are available on any firm in any free-world country. Prepared by Foreign Service officers, they describe the operations of the company and list products handled, manufacturers from whom it imports, size and reputation of the company, its capital and annual turnover, and other important facts.

Information about purchases being made by foreign firms and governments under International Cooperation Administration (ICA) foreign aid programs is disseminated by Field Offices.

If you have agents abroad, the Agency Index may assist you. This service, maintained by our Embassies and Consulates, lists names and addresses of local companies which carry products of specific U.S. Manufacturers. From this list, FS posts can direct other local businessmen to your agent.

And, as usual, Uncle Sam, your export assistant, is ready to flood you with more help and information.

There are several sources of clear, concise information about the necessary paperwork of overseas shipments:

World Trade Information Service reports entitled "Preparing Shipments to (country)" are available on most countries. Field Offices have supplementary information about the documents you need for any shipment to any country.

Special counseling and publications on techniques of shipping, such as the roles of freight forwarders, carriers, insurance companies, custom house brokers, banks, and others, and on export control regulations and procedures for securing necessary export licenses may be obtained at any Field Office.

Field Offices can supply all Department of Commerce forms needed in foreign trade and will assist you in completing them correctly.

Obviously, Uncle Sam is in two-way foreign trade with both feet and is ready to knock himself out to give you the benefit of it all. What does this mean? Well, as I see it, it means you can count your potential customers not in the thousands, or even millions . . . but in the *billions!*

In an earlier book of mine, *How I Made $1,000,000 in Mail Order*, published by Prentice-Hall, Inc., I brought out some pertinent points about selling overseas. While that book was directed to the mail-order business, the pointers are just as important for you, whether you manufacture or distribute and whether or not you consider yourself a mail-order firm.

I said in that book:

> Especially today—because of the Common Market—many of you should give a good deal of thought to overseas sales. And what is the "Common Market"? The Common Market is literally a "United States of Europe" that originally consisted of France, West Germany, Italy, The Netherlands, Belgium and Luxemburg. These countries formed a single economic union to serve 170 million European consumers and its success is beyond all expectations. Although the Common Market is only a few years old, by the end of 1961 all quota restrictions on trade in industrial goods between the six countries had been established, and before long it appears that merchandise will be able to move freely from one Common Market country to another without being hampered by tariffs, taxes or duties. The ultimate aim is to unite most of the European countries into a European Economic Federation with a total of 250 million people whose products and workers will be able to move as freely

across the national borders as we move across state
borders in the United States.

Now is the time to get your product distributed
in these Common Market countries and the working
tools described in this chapter can help you achieve
this goal. To many people the foreign market seems
remote and mysterious, but once you learn a few
basic marketing tricks, it's sometimes almost easier
to sell ten thousand units of your product to an importer in Milan, Italy, than ten dozen to a jobber
in Chicago. Quite often the same qualities that sell
your product in the U.S.A. will also find a ready and
willing market overseas. People are basically the same
throughout the world . . . usually what appeals to an
American father, mother and child, or average consumer will strike a responsive chord in their overseas
counterpart.

In that chapter I went on to touch on many of the
government sources of help we'll go over more fully
here. And the help is so unusually rich, it's hard to know
where to begin. Maybe a personal experience will show
you one way that this tremendous market can be tapped.

A case in point is our Cossman Fly Cake. Fly Cake
is a solid chemical, in the shape of a small doughnut, with
the incredible ability to kill flies a few seconds after
they touch the cake. Best of all, Cossman Fly Cake retains
its killing power for an entire season and is effective as
long as a single crumb remains. Because of these remarkable qualities, Fly Cake easily found a placein the American market, and we soon began searching for other
markets overseas.

Aside from a one-time experience in export selling
several years ago, we had no previous background in this

field. We were fortunate in selling 200,000 Cossman Fly Cakes to an organization in Australia, and this whetted our appetite for more of this lucrative business. One thing amazed us: the 200,000 Cossman Fly Cake order from Australia was no more complicated than selling a few gross to any one of our jobber accounts here in the United States. So, what did we do to get more of this foreign business? We contacted the Bureau of International Commerce in Washington, D. C., and asked their advice on how to get overseas agents for our products. The bureau referred us to their office in Los Angeles, and we couldn't believe our eyes when we made our first call there. The local Los Angeles office was a merchandising wonderland of ideas on how to get business overseas. Today, Cossman Fly Cake is sold in most of the major countries throughout the world, and I can truthfully say that a good part of our success in our world-wide distribution of Fly Cake is due to the help and assistance we received from the Department of Commerce. Let me tell you about a few of these services.

ACTIONS SPEAK LOUDER . . .

I've won many a drink from a smart businessman by betting him he couldn't name five of the actual pavement-pounding services the government offers the overseas trader. Can you?

Pick up a green booklet called *How the Bureau of Foreign Commerce Works for You* and note the many services available to you. (Incidentally, unless otherwise noted all references in this chapter are published by and available from the Bureau of International Commerce, which is part of the Department of Commerce; unless prices are quoted, they are free. Write to the Commerce Field Office nearest you. The list is in Chapter I.)

But back to the green booklet. Let's note a few of the services listed in it.

1. Need a Consulting Service?

Specialists in the Bureau of International Commerce cover most foreign countries on economic developments, regulations you'll have to follow, trade statistics, etc. Even old-timers in the field have plenty of need for these Bureau of International Commerce specialists, and a newcomer will find them a lifesaver. They help you to complete your picture of any country as far as buying your products is concerned, and they give you straight, factual answers to specific questions. It's almost like having high-ranking, top-level consulting specialists on your payroll —free.

2. Uncle Knocks on Doors for You

How'd you like a top American businessman—say the president of U.S. Steel or Xerox, or Continental Can— to go to work for *you* . . . for *free?* Pipe dreams? Ordinarily, yes. But wouldn't it be loverly?

All right, you can wake up . . . and it's true. Every year United States trade missions carry thousands of queries from American businessmen to foreign countries. The answers they bring back have helped many companies to find overseas markets for their products. These trade missions are actually top-level private business executives, working with government officials, who volunteer their services to promote United States trade abroad. They conduct on-the-spot discussions with foreign businessmen and find out exactly what they need and want. Each year twelve to fifteen of these missions visit twenty or more countries. Think what it would cost you to send a high-salaried, experienced representative to each of these twenty countries to find out whether it's worth while for you to make a pitch to that country for *your* products! Uncle Sam does all this spadework for the cost to you of a five-cent stamp!

HERE'S HOW IT WORKS. Let's say you're a toy manufacturer looking for new markets in foreign countries. First, check with your local Department of Commerce Field Office for countries scheduled for trade missions. Then answer the following nine questions by letter sent to your Field Office. (Where more than one country is scheduled there should be one original and two carbon copies of your letter for each foreign country).

1. Do you now have business connections or are you represented in any of these countries? (If you have an exclusive representative, the trade mission cannot locate another agent for you.) If you are represented, by whom and in which country (countries)?

2. Have you had previous business experience with these countries? List countries.

3. What products do you wish to sell or purchase and in which countries? Or, what type of business transactions do you wish to make? Describe products in detail.

4. Do you wish to obtain an agent or do you prefer to export directly? If so, in which countries?

5. Do you prefer to import for your own account or to act as an agent?

6. Will you consider direct investment or a joint venture, such as providing machinery, know-how, or capital with a qualified firm?

7. Are you interested in licensing a qualified company to produce your products abroad? If so,

describe in detail the nature of the agreement you would consider.

8. To what extent are you prepared to sell on long-term credit or, if dollar exchange is not available, accept payment in foreign currency?

9. What type of company would be qualified to transact your business?

Whatever pertinent information a company can provide will help the agents of the trade mission. This includes catalogues and brochures as well as information about the size and scope of a company's activities. No one is too large or too small to be represented.

When the trade mission get to the country in question, they will explore the market potential for you and scout for profitable export-import opportunities, agents or distributors, licensing possibilities, etc. And all this costs you the grand sum of a five-cent postage stamp. How can you beat it?

On the other side of the coin, the trade mission will also look for trade opportunities for you in the country they visit. For example, let's assume you wanted to represent a good perfume manufacturer from France. You would contact the trade mission leaving for France, tell them of your wishes, and when they get to France, they would literally knock on doors to locate a good company for you.

To get an idea of what a typical trade mission can do, look at a free copy of *Seven Americans in Peru,* which you can order from the Bureau of International Business Operations of the Bureau of International Commerce. Here's a small sample of the down-to-earth information brought back by this oneparticular trade mission. They found Peruvian businesses.

• Interested in installation of an offset printing plant with a one color press 18″ x 24″; Establecimientos Graficos L. Alfredo Nava S.A., San Juan de Dios 206, Arequipa.

• Interested in machinery to process cashew nuts, shelling, extracting cashew oil from shell and processing nuts. Productos Rey, S.A., Prol. Gamarra 661, Lima.

• Wishes to purchase a potato slicer to be used in the production of potato chips. Huancayo Tours, Puno 636, Apartado 545, Huancayo.

• Wishes to purchase color applied (baked-on) label machinery. Fabrica Vidrios San Isidro, Tacna 959, Chiclayo.

• Wants to establish small processing canning plant for pineapple with a capacity of 1200 tons per year. Would like to receive preliminary proposal for simplest possible machinery. Nemesio Maduana M., Santa Isabel 827, Huancayo.

• Wants proposal and technical advice on steam distillation of lemongrass. Hacienda Negro Urco Rio Napo, Apartado 102, Iquitos.

• Interested in receiving prices and literature for low cost drying equipment for coffee. Agricola Perucosa, Casilla 3553, Lima.

• Interested in proposal for a complete dairy plant with a production of 8000 liters per day. Banco Regional, Apartado 360, Huancayo.

• Interested in purchasing a complete poultry dressing plant. Instituto Sanitas Sociedad Peruana, Paseo Republica No. 119, Lima.

• Interested in plant to produce oxygen gas in cylinders and acetylene gas in cylinders; wants equipment to produce 2500 to 3000 kilos of oxygen. Edmundo Vizcarra R., Calle Beaterio 150, Arequipa.

• Interested in importing masonry machinery

for tiles, blocks, pipe, etc.; Dr. Juan Barandiaran, Jiron Arequipa 196, Lima.

These orders and many, many more are open for some American firm to fill—maybe yours!

3. Uncle's Date Bureau

This is the reverse of the foreign-trade mission. Responsible businessmen from other countries visiting the United States are invited to come to the Department of Commerce and use its facilities. Their names, firms, purpose of visit, time and place to contact them—all these are printed in *International Commerce.* So you can contact these businessmen from foreign lands without the expense of a business trip.

4. Unaccustomed as I Am

Maybe you can't speak on your feet, but the Bureau of International Commerce does it for you. The Bureau of International Commerce is the businessman's voice in the development of American foreign-trade policy. Both at home and abroad, bureau officials set forth the views of American world traders and help to promote their best interests. The bureau works to improve the world climate for American capital by co-operating with other countries and tearing down obstacles to investment. Tariffs, export and import controls, transportation, communications, utilities, currency, property rights, customs regulations, insurance, loans and investment, arbitration of trade disputes—these are the areas in which the bureau is your world spokesman.

5. Want a Foreign Agent?

Not the cloak-and-dagger type, of course, but a representative for your product abroad. A special service in your field is available to help you find agents or distributors in foreign countries to sell your products. If you have been unable to make satisfactory trade connections through regular sources of information supplied by the Bureau of International Commerce—Trade Lists, Trade Opportunities, World Trade Directory reports, and other media—you may apply for a Trade Contact Survey.

WHAT THE SERVICE IS. A Trade Contact Survey is a specialized, professional service designed to locate several foreign firms in a particular country which meet your specific requirements and which express an interest in the representation you offer. It is conducted "on the spot' by a Foreign Service officer at the request of BIC.

TIME REQUIRED. A survey is usually completed in about sixty days. The time is subject to difficulty encountered in locating suitable prospects but an interim report will be supplied.

RESULTS OF SURVEY. You will receive a summary report of the information developed, including pertinent marketing data as well as the names and addresses of qualified prospects. Individual World Trade Directory reports giving background information on these firms are also furnished. If the Foreign Service officer has been unable to locate any firms interested in the proposal or if the particular operation planned is not feasible the reasons will be explained in the report and possible alternate suggestions offered.

PRICE. A charge of $10.00 is made for each survey conducted.

HOW TO APPLY. Ask the Department of Commerce

Field Office in your area to supply you with copies of form FC-963, Application for Assistance in Selecting an Agent or Distributor Abroad. Members of the Field Office staff will also assist you in preparing the forms. Or you may write to the Commercial Intelligence Division, Bureau of International Commerce, U.S. Department of Commerce, Washington 25, D.C.

There are the five services to win the bet. But we haven't begun to tap Uncle's capacity to help! Let's look at a few more.

6. Need a Mailing List of Prospective Foreign Customers?

Trade Lists identify firms handling specific commodities in foreign countries and cover a wide range of products, trades, and services. These lists contain the basic information needed to locate customers, agents, distributors, licensees, and sources of supply abroad. In addition to a listing of firms, each Trade List contains a summary of basic trade and industry data, a brief analysis of foreign trade in the commodity, government regulations affecting trade, and other useful market data. Lists of importers and dealers indicate the relative size of each firm, method of operation, products handled, territory, and sales force. Lists of exporters and manufacturers indicate relative size or production capacity of each firm and name the products handled. Trade Lists are $2.00 each per country.

7. Want to Draw a Credit Report on a Foreign Company?

World Trade Directory Reports contain business particulars on individual foreign firms. These reports, which complement the trade-list service, supply the detailed information needed to determine the competence and general reliability of specific foreign firms. They are prepared by the American Foreign Service and represent a consensus of reliable sources of information. If the report on file is more than a year old, a revised current report is prepared without additional charge. The complete name and address of the foreign firm should be given when ordering World Trade Directory Reports. These reports cost only $1.00 each.

8. Looking for a Foreign Advertising Agency?

One of the best sources of information is the Department of Commerce's book entitled *A Directory of Foreign Advertising Agencies and Marketing Research Organizations*. This *Directory* costs only 45 cents but is worth many many times that amount. It gives detailed information on advertising agencies and marketing research organizations in most of the civilized countries of the world.

9. Want a List of Foreign Business Directories?

Again, contact your Department of Commerce and buy their book, *A Guide to Foreign Business Directories*. This *Guide* is intended for businessmen seeking to identify persons or companies engaging in commerce, a specific industry, or a profession in other countries. The *Guide* is presented in two principal parts:

(*a*) The first part, *Country Directories*, contains the titles of directories published in or dealing with countries of the free world. These countries are arranged alphabetically.

(*b*) The second principal part of the *Guide* lists directories alphabetically by industry, trade, or profession. Here in one volume you'll find information on directories of importers, manufacturers, suppliers, exporters, trade associations, individual professional and businessmen, and government officials. It also gives you the names and addresses of each directory's publisher, where to get the directory, and the price.

10. A Little Bit of Home

If you import or export, or even manufacture an article using a foreign part or ingredient, you'll do well to look into the little-known "Free Port" or Foreign Trading Zone system. These ports are spotted all over the trading world. American vacationers who have stopped at the famous Shannon free port where Irish whisky can be bought without paying duty can testify to at least one of these benefits! The United States has six of these ports: at Staten Island, Seattle, New Orleans, Toledo, San Francisco, and one in Puerto Rico.

More and more, businessmen are becoming aware of the advantages of the system. A small manufacturer unable to afford overseas facilities otherwise can now use the ports as a money-saving alternative. The Foreign Trade Zones Board publishes a booklet you can get for 30 cents, entitled *Laws, Regulation, and Other Information Relating to Foreign Trade Zones in the United States.* Unfortunately, the text is just as stuffy as the title, but it's worth the effort of reading when thousands of dollars may be saved by understanding what it has to say. The basic idea of the free port is that goods deposited or manufactured in the free-port area are technically not considered to have entered the United States and are therefore not subject to import duty unless and until they actually cross into the United States proper. The booklet also explains some of the other free-port privileges.

A beautiful provision of the system is that you pay duty only on the merchandise "weight" actually imported. Taking advantage of this, a friend of mine saved $20,000 on a shipment of Brazil nuts. The unripe nuts waited in the Staten Island port for several months while the moisture content dropped from 50 per cent to less than 10 per cent. Thus, he was spared paying up to a cent and a half a pound for pure water! This is watering the stock, in reverse!

TRAVEL IS BIG BUSINESS . . .

The Department of Commerce has the job, among many others, of promoting tourist trade. Naturally, the travel industry is delighted to co-operate. Other countries are encouraged to let down bars that hamper the travel of Americans abroad, and we likewise encourage visits by foreign vacationers. In recent years you see more and more advertisements and posters in European countries, inviting Frenchmen, Englishmen, Italians, etc., to visit the Grand Canyon and Disneyland. This traffic is on the increase and every visitor is a potential customer. Maybe for you!

THE WATER'S FINE! . . .

Have I convinced you that Uncle Sam doesn't stop with the printed word when it comes to helping you do business overseas? That doesn't mean that he's shy on literature in this field. So let's take a look at some of the publications you can get on foreign trade.

As a starter, go back to the book we quoted in the preceding chapter, the *Directory of Foreign Organizations*. The free publicity you can get for appropriate trade notices and inquiries is fantastic. For instance, if you have something to interest English businessmen, you can reach 26,500 British firms with a *free* notice by sending it to just *three* journals! That's the combined membership of the London Chamber of Commerce monthly *Commerce*, the *FBI Journal* (of the Federation of British Industries), and the *British Manufacturer*. Similar opportunities are open in many other countries. Consult the *Directory* for the nation you are interested in.

If you've never looked into import-export, you can get the full story in the handbook put out by the Foreign Commerce Department of the Chamber of Commerce, Washington 6, D.C. It's called *An Introduction to Doing Import and Export Business*. It costs $2.00 and is worth a thousand times the price. While not a government agency, the Chamber of Commerce is of course the next thing to one and gives you the same full, impartial, and objective kind of service. This 136-page book takes up importing and exporting and each of the topics is fleshed out in detail. For instance the subheadings on the chapter entitled "the Import Order" include:

Essential Considerations.
The Quotation: Price; Currency of Quotation; Weights and Measures; Quality Guarantees; Foreign Trade Definitions; Method of Payment.
Other Terms of Purchase.
Arbitration.
Packing.
Marking.
Import Documents.
  Invoices
  Statement of Charges
  Packing List
  Inspection of Analysis Certificate
  Bill of Lading
  Insurance Policy
Forwarding of Documents.

I have found this book handy for quick reference on all my own overseas transactions.

For the government treatment of the over-all picture, turn to *Guides for the Newcomer to World Trade*, published by the BIC for 15 cents. It is especially valuable in referring you to other publications put out by the BIC and the Business and Defense Services Administration. The specialists in this BDSA gather, sift, and pass out information on the commercial activity in many specific industries. Here are some of the subscriptions you can order.

Chemical and Rubber. Monthly. $1.75 a year. Presents production trends, sales, inventories, outlook for selected commodities, foreign developments, and special analyses of specific chemical and rubber products.

Containers and Packaging. Quarterly. 75 cents a year. Reviews current and near-future trends of these industries. Contains analyses and all data on production, consumption, inventories, exports, imports, and current and future trends and includes occasional special articles on foreign markets for packaging materials and equipment.

Copper. Quarterly. 50 cents a year. Presents statistical data and analyses covering such subjects as requirements for and distribution of copper-base raw materials as well as for mill and foundry products, exports and imports of copper, and shipments and unfulfilled orders of brass mill and copper wire mill products.

Pulp, Paper and Board. Quarterly. 75 cents a year. Reviews current and future trends, sales, inventories, wholesale distribution, employment, prices, and other related factors.

Foreign-trade participation by the Department of State, Department of Agriculture, the Customs Bureau, Food and Drug Administration, and others are also covered in this booklet. But before we leave BDSA, we should mention that this bureau also publishes a general information booklet by the title of *What You Should Know about Exporting*. The cost is 25 cents. In addition, you can get books on specific areas, such as *The Market for Automatic Vending Machines in Austria* (25 cents) and *Electric Current Abroad* (also 25 cents).

For more detail and background information, the BIC publishes a *Checklist of BFC Publications*. It's free for the asking, and the most recent issue will contain up-to-the minute trade reports that can be obtained from more than 290 Foreign Service Posts throughout the world. The trade reports and market research are analyzed, correlated, and supplemented by BIC's own specialists.

Listing the most current and useful books and pamphlets, the *Checklist* gives information on all phases of market-research data for foreign trade. Here are a few examples.

Information Sources on International Travel. Twelve mimeographed listings of basic source material for use by the international travel industry and the general traveling public. Check list and order form available from U.S. Department of Commerce, Washington 25, D.C., and its Field Offices.

Investment Handbooks. A series designed to assist both exporters and investors in marketing abroad. Describes basic conditions and economic outlook for a particular country, giving comprehensive data on the country's natural resources, industry, transport, communications, power facilities, finance, taxation, business methods, and trade and the government's attitude toward private foreign investment.

Seasonal Patterns of United States Travel Abroad. An analysis of quarterly periods of United States overseas travel. Presents detailed information on number of travelers (for specific years), purpose, means of transportation, and other travel factors for selected aeas. 54 pages. 20 cents.

Sending Gift Packages. Nearly every country in the world is covered in this series of circulars describing United States and foreign-country regulations on what can be included in a gift package, what senders should know about packaging regulations, what the recipient must do to receive gift packages, and what he must pay. Available from the United States Department of Commerce, Washington 25, D.C., and its Field Offices. 10 cents per country report.

Sources of Credit Information on Foreign Firms. A guide to reference sources of foreign credit information in the United States and abroad. 84 pages. 30 cents.

Sources of Information on Foreign Trade Practice. A guide to the principal reference sources giving the exporter and importer fundamental information on foreign-trade techniques. 47 pages. 25 cents.

Survey of International Travel. Assembles basic facts and figures about the United States' share in the growing business of international travel. Traces the pattern and expenditures for travel since such statistics were first recorded by the United States Government. Includes a list of foreign tourist information offices in the United States and selected references. 63 pages. 35 cents.

After all this, the booklet takes up more than a hundred nations, country by country, showing the material you can receive on each one.

Another booklet to guide you through the profitable foreign-trade maze is: *Sources of Information on Foreign Trade Practice,* 25 cents. This booklet lists the Commerce publications as well as over three hundred other titles from *all* public and private sources.

The BIC also publishes that wonderful periodical, *International Commerce.* This weekly magazine offers practical, authoritative, and concise international marketing information and news and reports demonstrating and explaining potential advantages to American businessmen in profitable international sales of United States products around the world, in the easily read form of a weekly news magazine. It carries feature articles on significant developments in the United States export-trade expansion and other programs, the accomplishments of United States trade missions, analyses of United States and foreign trade, and reports on outstanding activities of such organizations as GATT, the Common Market, Eximbank, the World Bank, ECAFE, and ECSC. (Annual subscription: $16.00; $5.00 additional for foreign mailing.) Make your remittance payable to the Superintendent of Documents and mail either to a Department of Commerce Field Office or to the Superintendent of Documents, U.S. Government Printing Office, Washington, D.C., 20402. A single copy is free as a sample; otherwise single copies cost 35 cents each.

Articles by experts are sandwiched between opportunity tips on world trade. For example, the issue open in front of me contains a special report on seven hundred trade fairs being held in sixty-one countries whose doors are open to American exhibitors and vendors. Business-outlook articles and the latest word on government actions here and abroad fill out the publication. Here is part of the table of contents of a recent issue:

SPECIAL REPORTS—East Africa: a Common Market Open to U.S. Goods.

Features
Hearings Underway on Items for GATT Negotiations
Neil Hurley's Column
'E' Award Winners Near Total of 400

Trade Fairs and Centers
Household Goods Show Scheduled in Cologne
Specialized Hotel Equipment Fair to Be Held in Paris

Worldwide Business Outlook
Wave of Optimism Carries Ecuador's Economy
Venezuelan Upturn Continues Despite Pre-election Lull

U.S. Government Actions
California, Chile form Partnership under Alliance

Foreign Government Actions
Syria Imposes More Taxes on Imported Cinema Films

Investment Opportunities
Final East African List Shows Area's Great Potential
Private Aid Sought for Pakistan Projects

World Trade Opportunities
Variety of Equipment Sought in Several Countries
New Trade Lists; Visiting Buyers and Officials
Leads for Exporters
Special Trade Leads
International Representation
Leads for Importers
Construction Projects

As a sample of the very usable information you may expect to find between these covers, a recent article headed "Interest of U.S. Exporters in Swedish Textile Market Picks Up" by the commercial attaché at Stockholm, Mr. Gustave E. Larson, sent a friend of mine racing to get more information about selling his line of sports clothes in Sweden, an idea that had never occurred to him before. He got all the information he needed through a trade mission and was put in touch with a responsible firm willing and anxious to act as his Swedish distributor. A year later he racked up over a quarter-million dollars in sales from this unexpected market, which also led him to many other European countries as potential customers.

THE RED CARPET . . .

There's a big dessert at the end of this foreign-trade banquet sponsored, hosted, and catered by your Uncle Sam. It's this: If you really jump into the big foreign market, sooner or later you'll find yourself traveling to some of the countries where you've done business or corresponded. In my book, *How I Made $1,000,000 in Mail Order*, I told how I was wined, dined, and treated like royalty on my first trip over, driven around in Rolls-Royces, introduced to the biggest business tycoons . . . and all through the contacts made with the help of the BIC and the other agencies I've been beating the drum about throughout this chapter. It can happen to you, too! It doesn't matter if your office is a hole in the wall or a corner of your kitchen table; the foreign contacts are made through your impressive letterhead, and for all that your business friends abroad know, you could buy and sell General Motors three times a day. What's the moral? Simply this: *You don't have to be a big man to do big business!*

All right. Fifteen billion dollars worth of goods are sold abroad annually by American businessmen. Get busy and grab *your* share!

BIBLIOGRAPHY

Chamber of Commerce of the United States, Foreign Commerce Department. *An Introduction to Doing Import and Export Business.* $2.00.

Foreign-Trade Zones Board. *Laws, Regulations, and Other Information Relating to Foreign-Trade Zones in the United States.* 30 cents.

Small Business Administration. *Export Marketing for Smaller Firms.* 50 cents.

———. *Pointers on International Trade.*

U.S. Department of Agriculture. *Foreign Agriculture (Including Foreign Crops and Markets) Weekly.* $5.50 per year.

U.S. Department of Commerce. (Booklets.)

U.S. Business Participation in Trade Fairs Abroad. 15 cents.

Sources of Information on Foreign Trade Practice. 25 cents.

Electric Current Abroad. 25 cents.

The U.S. Trade Missions Program.

A Directory of Foreign Development Organizations for Trade and Investment. 30 cents.

Channels for Trading Abroad. 25 cents.

A Directory of Foreign Organization for Trade and Investment Promotion. 35 cents.

———. *How the Bureau of Foreign Commerce Works for You.*

———. *International Commerce—"Trade Fairs" Issue.*

———. *Report of the U.S. Department of Commerce: U.S. Resources and Trade Development Mission to Peru—"Seven Americans in Peru."*

———. Bureau of Foreign Commerce. *Checklist of BFC Publications.* 15 cents.

———. *A Directory of Foreign Advertising Agen-*

cies and Marketing Research Organizations. 45 cents.

————. *A Guide to Foreign Business Directories.* 45 cents.

————. *Guides for the Newcomer to World Trade.* 15 cents.

————. *World Trade Review (Foreign Commerce Weekly Supplement).* $6.00 per year.

————. Commercial Intelligence Division. *Aids for American Foreign Traders.*

U.S. Department of Commerce, Office of Field Services Bureau of Foreign Commerce. *Services Available to U.S. Exporters.*

U.S. Department of International Commerce. *International Commerce (Weekly).* $16.00 per year; single copy 35 cents.

U.S. Department of State. *Foreign Consular Offices in the United States.* 30 cents.

————, Bureau of Administration. Office of Personnel. *Foreign Service List.* 60 cents.

CHAPTER V

UNCLE SAM AS YOUR IDEA MAN

INCREASING YOUR PROFITS
WITH GOVERNMENT HELP

Next to your wife, there's no one more anxious to see you get ahead in your business than that Uncle of yours. He has a million ideas for you to use and is begging you to take them, free. Let's look into some of the tricks he has up his sleeve to increase your profits.

WOULD YOU LIKE FREE USE OF A GOVERNMENT-OWNED INVENTION?

You are welcome to it. That's right: the patented ideas of hundreds of thousands of inventors are all yours for the asking. The patents belong to the government, which asks no royalty from you.

Where does this free bonanza come from? Well, many are patents and processes and products developed by the government itself, through its many research laboratories. If General Electric or Remington-Rand had developed the ideas, they'd belong to the proper corporations and would be out of your reach. But because the government scientists created them, they're offered to you on a royalty-free license.

Other patents are "dedicated," that is, given to the

government by civic-minded business firms and individuals. We learn that when a patent is dedicated the inventor gives up all ownership and control of the invention. Therefore, no license to make, use or sell the invention is required, and no royalty need be paid.

Just to cite a few important products originating through government research and development: There's the remote control for television sets (which came as a result of remote-control command systems for missiles and satellites); also the electronic wrist watch. Of course, you don't get exclusive use; anyone else is free to take up the same idea. Chances are, however, that he'll use it differently and in a way that doesn't compete with you. That's because most of the ideas need imagination and initiative to make them commercial. Few of these patents are ready for the market "as is," but a little engineering work and a lot of sales know-how will develop many of them into profitable products to add to your own line.

These ideas are briefly described in the free Patent Abstract Series, published by the Office of Technical Services, Department of Commerce. This is a series of publications designed to inform the business public of patented inventions owned by the government which are ordinarily available for license to private firms on a royalty-free basis. Many small and large companies are now manufacturing products or using processes covered by government-owned patents or developed through further engineering work based on such government patents.

Reading a few of the different items listed in these books will give you some idea of the sales possibilities opened up in this idea grab bag. They cover toys, sporting goods, athletic supplies, pens, pencils, costume jewelry, novelties and notions, clocks and watches—to name only a few. In one of these lists, we found an improved earphone-socket design which we adapted and sold to television, radio, and tape-recorder listeners at a nice profit.

If you want more information about any of the inventions, you can get the complete specifications and claims made for the device or process for 25 cents from the Commissioner of Patents, Department of Commerce. And when you decided to use one of the inventions, you apply to the government agency which is listed as administrator of the patent. This will usually be one of the Cabinet Departments (Commerce, Defense, or Agriculture), but in some cases it may be administered by the Tennessee Valley Authority, the Atomic Energy Commission, GSA, or the Federal Power Commission.

MORE PATENTS . . . BUT NOT FREE . . .

While we're on the subject of patents, we must not forget the 1,200 patents that are granted *each week* to inventors. We'll talk about how you can secure a patent on a device or process of your own invention later in this book. Here, I want to talk about other people's patents. Every one of them, of course, was patented in the fervent hope that you or some other businessman would offer to buy, rent, or pay a royalty on it. These new patents are described as they come out in the Patent Office's weekly *Official Gazette*. Besides describing newly granted patents (with illustrations), it lists patents available for licensing or sale, reports news of patent suits, lists new trade-mark registrations, and gives other information you may want to know about. Your local library probably has a copy. If 1,200 patents a week seems like a lot, remember the two fellows who looked out over the ocean. "Big, ain't it?" said one. "Sure is," said the other, "and you're only seeing the top of it!"

The new patents you see listed in the *Official Gazette* are only the surface of the literally millions of patents available. To read about these, you'll have to go to the Patent Office in Washington or to one of the repository libraries in a number of larger cities. (The Patent Office in Washington or your own public library will tell you where the nearest one is located.)

A personal experience will give you an idea of the value of this ocean of business opportunities. After an evening at the symphony, watching the players turn pages of music, I thought that there might be a market for an automatic page turner to be used by musicians. At the patent room of the Los Angeles Public Library an obliging clerk helped me run down inventions already patented. There were a dozen or more. Many of them were so complicated that it would be impossible to make them, much less sell them; but I did find one that was light and simple and looked as if it could be brought in at a realistic price. I got in touch with the inventor, who had had no luck in merchandising his invention. He'd made a stab at selling his baby and had got nowhere. I made a deal for his tooling, putting him on a royalty. Advertising in the music magazines, we sold 12,000 of the devices at $7.95, making both the inventor and me quite happy.

The moral is: if you need a product not yet on the market, don't assume there is no such thing. Try the resources of the Patent Office first.

STILL MORE PATENTS . . .

Just one last word on another little-known source of *free* ideas. That's the storehouse of over 100,000 different items of technical know-how our government acquired as war reparations from German and Japanese laboratory and factory records and enemy-owned patents. Added to this are some of the results of United States wartime research that have been opened to public use without charge. Write to the Office of Technical Services for information on this free bonanza of ideas.

I recently developed and am now manufacturing a plastic frogman that swims under its own power for thirty minutes or more on a single fuel pellet. And where did I find the pellet? In a German patent that our government acquired after World War II! The patent gave details about a harmless chemical that created a steady stream of carbon dioxide when mixed with water. We merely took the formula, combined it into a small fuel pellet, and it will soon be propelling our plastic frogman into one of the top toy products in the country today . . . and our total development cost for the fuel propellent was a letter to the Office of Technical Services! Incidentally, we also used this same formulation in a fishing lure that swims under its own power for one hour or more, and which became another one of our winners!

A *last* word on patents: A publication called *Products List Circular* put out monthly by the SBA (free), lists not only privately owned and government-owned patents but also those patents which are expiring at the end of their 14- or 28-year period—your chance to pick up an invention in "public domain" whch you will not have to buy or lease but may use absolutely free. To save you from wading through a lot of useless material, the Small Business Administration selects the patents which have the most commercial possibilities. Many gift and giveaway items are featured. Here are some typical products from one issue:

Antenna Clip
Cabinet Support
Fastening Device
Headset
Ear Pads
Battery-Charging System
Door Latch
Electric Fence Post
Eraser Cleaner
Receptacle for Lipstick
    Holders and Lipsticks
Screen for Picture Projection
Skirt Rack
Baby-Bottle Holder

Collapsible Pet-Animal House
Fishing Implement
Automobile-Headlight
    Control Devices
Folding Flashlight Holder
Fishing-Rod Holder
Combination Toilet-Tissue
    Roll and Deodorant
    Container
Rodent Exterminator
Inflatable Hat
Razor-Blade Holder
Cigarette Holder
Hide-A-Way Door Stop

GOVERNMENT RESEARCH AT YOUR FINGERTIPS . . .

The creative thinking of the nation is piled up not only in patents but in research, and much of it belonging to the government is yours to use. Send $15.00 for an annual subscription to the twice-a-month *Research Reports* put out by the Office of Technical Services (Commerce). For $1.00 you can buy single copies of government reports on products, processes, and investigations that may be useful to your business.

Most of these reports are highly technical. But even a layman can understand the importance of an Army Medical Research Study on the digestibility and acceptability of a new dehydrated ration. Maybe this item, under a name like "Fruit-Flakies," could be the next blockbuster in the breakfast-food industry! But certainly, if you have anything to do with electronics, machinery, medicine, photography, or transportation, there may be something here for you.

Still on technical research, and perhaps a little closer to earth for the average businessman, is the *Technical Reports Newsletter* put out monthly by the Office of Technical Services. A typical issue will have ten or a dozen one-paragraph summaries of items directly useful to business.

And don't forget the previously mentioned *Marketing Information Guide*. Here are some listings I found in just one issue of this invaluable magazine:

> Bankruptcy Causes and Remedies
> The Products Liability Problem
> Patent Attorneys and Agents Available to Represent Inventors Before the U.S. Patent Office
> Marketing Food Products in American Samoa
> Foreign Publications and their United States Representatives
> United States Foreign Trade in Photographic Goods
> U.S. Trade with Japan: A Commodity Analysis
> 1200 Leading U.S. Corporations
> Basic Facts About the Carpet and Rug Industry
> Buyers' Guide-Directory of Equipment for Fire Departments
> Directory of the Plastics Industry
> Florida Electronics Directory
> The Plastic Foam Industry
> Improving Office Procedures in Food Brokers' Firms
> Marketing Through Food Brokers
> Frozen Food Handling
> Suburban Shopping Centers

One single entry from this publication put me onto a market for items I'd been selling only by mail up to then. This was the *Blue Book of Direct Selling*, a 16-page list of direct-selling firms. Through this list I was put in touch with several house-to-house distributors who took on my products as a side line for their salesmen. All of us—the companies, the salesmen, and I—reaped a healthy profit.

Many other listings put out by private associations are mentioned in the *Marketing Information Guides*. A hotel buyers' directory, or a directory of Florida industries, a museum directory of the United States and Canada, a list of 1,273 merchandise warehouses, an American church yearbook—these are all listings *on the same page* from which I picked the direct-selling *Blue Book*. If these don't strike a special spark with you, keep looking. You're bound to run into ideas you never dreamed of—ideas that will put money in your pocket.

SBA AGAIN . . .

Remember the Management Aids? We discussed them earlier in Chapters I and II as tools to choose and build a business. Let's pull out the list again and go over the titles once more, this time thinking of them as a *source of ideas*. Here are a few titles right off the top of the pile.

> *New Product Development and Sale*
> *Containers and Packaging*
> *Buying a Small Going Concern*
> *How Big Companies Help Small Marketers*
> *Methods for Improving Off-Season Sales*
> *Two Dozen Ideas for Effective Administration*
> *Mailing-List Houses*
> *Building Growth-Mindedness Into Your Business*

If I haven't already mentioned it, you can get a complete list of titles with order blanks from the SBA without cost. Before leaving this series, I want to suggest that you especially look into SBA Management Series pamphlet No. 25, *Guides for Profit Planning* (25 cents). It helps you decide whether your earnings and profits are reasonable in your present situation. If they are too low, it suggests how to guide future action for the greatest profit possibilities.

The booklet is a step-by-step explanation to help you understand what the big concerns call "profit control." They couldn't exist without it, and neither can you. Until you really know your break-even point, for instance, you can't really tell whether your business is in the red or in the black. The 50-page booklet tells you how to prepare your own break-even chart and gives you all the items of cost, both fixed and variable, you'll have to figure into it. It shows you how to analyze profit by several different yardsticks. And of course, like all government books, it ends with a listing of books, periodicals, and professional and business associations that will help you still further to understand this vital part of business.

IDEAS ARE WHERE YOU FIND THEM . . .

You must have noticed how other departments besides the Department of Commerce are getting into the act of helping you, the businessman. They're doing it right now. For example: The Department of Health, Education, and Welfare puts out a directory of 3,660 *libraries* which will lend or rent you literally hundreds of thousands of films (16-mm) on every subject under the sun. The directory was put together for teachers, librarians, and community groups; but what a source of ideas for the businessman! It will cost you $1.00. Write to the HEW's Office of Education.

Want to get more customers into your store? From this source alone, you could run a different film every day for two years without repeating one of them!

The *Federal Handbook for Small Business* is a survey of small-business programs of various government departments. It's put out by the Senate Select Committee on Small Business, the House Committee, the White House Committee, and the SBA, all co-operating. You can get it, free, from the Superintendent of Documents. A run-through of this book is like opening the door to a treasure vault of business help. The first chapter covers the SBA. We find a number of services we have already described in this book and some we'll take up in later chapters. Business loans, foreign-trade help, buying from the government, and selling to the government are all mentioned. Many SBA publications are suggested for reading.

Going into other government agencies, the *Handbook* comes up with the idea-sparking suggestions on every page. Let's take a few examples.

1. One branch of the Commerce Department we haven't mentioned up to now is the National Bureau of Standards. Many of this agency's programs benefit small business directly or indirectly. The bureau operates a Building Research Program. If you happen to run a small construction firm without money to spend investigating building materials and structural safety, your government has done it for you. If you have any questions about standards of any kind, a letter to the Bureau of Standards, Washington, D.C., will flood you with information you can count on.

2. If you run a small business and want your employees to have more training, the government will do

the job for you. Startling? It's true. The *Handbook* informs us that the Department of Labor will actually train apprentices and other workers in tool and die, printing and publishing, and many other industries.

For additional information on this amazing program, write the Department of Labor, Washington, D.C., for these publications:

National Apprenticeship Program
Trade and Industry (Nos. 1 through 7)
National Apprenticeship Standards (for your particular business field or locality)
People . . . Production . . . Profits
Follow-Up Study of Former Apprentices

3. Continuing through the *Handbook*, we find that the Department of the Interior offers topographical maps and information on geological, mineral, and water resources. The Geological Survey has a library of over 100,000 photographs you can buy.

4. The Bureau of Mines (Interior) will keep you informed on health and safety problems of the mineral industry, as well as useful processes for mining, extracting and using minerals, metals, and fuels.

5. Did you know that your government will grubstake you for a prospecting expedition? It's a fact! We quote:

> The Office of Minerals Exploration offers financial assistance to firms and individuals who desire to explore their properties or claims for certain mineral commodities. This help is offered to applicants who ordinarily would not undertake the exploration under present conditions or circumstances at their sole ex-

pense and who are unable to obtain funds from commercial sources on reasonable terms.

The Government will contract with an eligible applicant to pay up to one-half of the cost of approved exploration work. The Government's share may not exceed $250,000 per contract. The operator (applicant) does the work, pays the bills, and submits a monthly report of the work done and costs incurred.

An Office of Minerals Exploration field officer inspects and approves acceptable work, after which the Government reimburses the operator for one-half of the aceptable costs. The operator's time spent on the work and charges for the use of equipment which he owns may be applied toward his share of the cost.

Funds contributed by the Government are repaid by a 5-percent royalty on production from the property. If nothing is produced, there is no obligation to repay.

If this interests you, get in touch with the Office of Minerals Exploration, Department of the Interior, Washington, D.C., or one of the Department's Regional Offices.

6. Many other bureaus of the Interior offer financial, research, or other profit-boosting aids in the fields of timber, fisheries, and land management. The National Park Service points out that with the tremendous increase in popularity of the various national parks, more and more opportunities are open for hotels, restaurants, motels, garages, and shops of all kinds to service the crowds, both as concessions inside the parks and on the roads leading to them.

7. Ever dream of the lazy life on a tropic Bali H'ai? The Trust Territory of the Pacific Islands provides loans

to locally owned private enterprises. To request further information as to procedures, write to High Commissioner of the Trust Territory of the Pacific Islands, Saipan, Marianas.

The Virgin Islands Government has a tax-incentive program to attract industry, including small light industry. For detailed procedures write to Commissioner, Department of Commerce, Government of the Virgin Islands, St. Thomas, Virgin Islands.

The Government of Guam has business-tax exemptions for manufacturers and producers. For detailed procedures write to Commissioner, Department of Commerce, Agana, Guam.

The Government of American Samoa has a tax-incentive program to attract industry, including small light industry. For detailed procedures write to Governor of American Samoa, Pago Pago, Tutuila, American Samoa.

Well, what more can you ask? Uncle Sam may draw the line at providing you with a golden-skinned beauty for the housekeeping, but short of that . . . it's ask, and ye shall receive!

8. It's not what you make; it's what you keep after taxes that counts. And the Internal Revenue Service wants you to keep every dollar you're legally entitled to. To help the small businessman with his tax problems, the IRS puts out a Mr. Businessman Kit and has other services tailored for you. Still quoting from the *Handbook*, here's how they describe the service:

A Mr. Businessman's Kit has been developed for presentation to operators of new businesses as they are formed. Its purpose primarily is to encourage more effective voluntary compliance by helping new businessmen to become fully aware of their responsibilities for filing all the Federal tax returns for which they may be liable, and for paying the taxes due. The Kit is a four-pocket folder designed to hold forms and instructions for preparing most business tax returns. On each pocket is a list of the various forms and documents applicable to the particular business. It also contains a check list of tax returns, a calendar of due dates for filing returns and paying taxes, a convenient place to keep employment tax information for employers, and a pocket for keeping retained copies of tax returns and related materials.

The principal feature of this program, however, is the *personal* presentation of the kit to the taxpayer. Internal Revenue Officers will present the kits and explain the various forms and documents applicable to the particular business. Thus each kit is tailored to the needs of the taxpayer.

The Revenue Officer will make every effort to assist and advise the businessman of his tax filing requirements. A place has been provided on the kit for the Revenue Officer's name, address and telephone number. The businessman will be encouraged to contact the Revenue Officer at any time to obtain further assistance or information.

Tax Guide for Small Business . . .

The Internal Revenue Service publishes annually a *Tax Guide for Small Business* which explains federal tax problems for sole proprietors, partners, partnerships, and corporations.

Income, excise, and employment taxes are explained in nontechnical language, and many examples are used to illustrate the application of the tax laws.

A check list, of particular interest to the new businessman, shows at a glance the taxes for which different kinds of business organizations and business activities may be liable and what the businessman should do about them.

A tax calendar is included, which explains, on a day-by-day basis, what the businessman should do in regard to his federal taxes and when he should do it. The two pages may be removed from the booklet and posted in a prominent place as a reminder of the various tax-due dates for the taxes discussed.

Establishing a new business, purchasing a going concern, operating a business, organizing a partnership and corporation, the sale of a business as a unit, the dissolution of a partnership, and the liquidation of a corporation are among the subjects covered in detail in the booklet.

The publication is revised annually to include new rules and changes in tax laws, regulations, and rulings. Plain language is used in the text; supplemented by many examples explaining such things as the need for adequate records and how long they should be retained; employee expense accounts; self-employment tax; declaration of expenses; bad debts; rental expenses and leases; depreciation; educational expenses; how to compute net profit; the cost of goods sold and inventories.

The booklet is available at local Internal Revenue Service offices. It may also be ordered from the Superintendent of Documents, U.S. Government Printing Office, Washington, D.C. 20402, for 40 cents a copy. Quantities of one hundred or more may be purchased for 30 cents a copy from the Superintendent of Documents.

OTHER VEINS TO TAP . . .

If you've stayed with me this far, I hope I've pretty well convinced you of one thing: that you can save time, money, and elbow grease by doing a little reading before you leap into any business plan.

Sounds so simple, you'd think any businessman in his right mind would be doing it automatically. Unfortunately, that's not true. A business executive told me at lunch one day that his organization had spent over $10,000 in travel, research, and high-priced consultation fees to track down a basic fact. "But," he said proudly, "it was money well spent. We plan to base our whole long-range business efforts on this fact."

I'd been collecting and studying government books and pamphlets for years as a hobby and as a necessary tool in my own business (that's how I came to write this book!). My friend's remark nagged at my memory. When I got back to my office I rummaged through my files. You guessed it! I mailed him the little pamphlet he could have bought for a dime, containing all the information he had so expensively and painfully rounded up. He'd never stopped to think that maybe somebody had gone through it all before.

The moral should be self-evident. Never, never, *never* make an important business move without first running a "literature search." This book gives you some idea of the vast resources of the United States Government. However, I'd be shortchanging you if I left you with the impression that Uncle Sam in the *only* rich, generous, and helpful Uncle you have.

Let's make a little detour here and outline some, not all, of the other stockpiles of business information at your command, especially if you live in or near a reasonably large city.

1. State and Municipal Sources

Very much like the federal government, many state, county, and city governments put out reams of printed information. Some of this, being narrower in range and closer to home, may actually be *more* useful to your business than federal information which covers the whole country. You can get state directories on local industrial problems, statistics on car and truck registration, school population, tax collections, maps, employment and unemployment, public health (the possibilities are endless) by writing to the public-relations department in your state capital, county seat, or city hall.

2. Colleges and Universities

Most colleges and universities publish books, periodicals, and other useful material and will furnish title lists on request. The large universities with a school of business administration will have built up stockpiles of business and research information you'll find very valuable. Again, the material is very likely to be gathered close to home, making the information that much more useful to you.

3. Magazines

This time I'm talking about general-circulation magazines as well as business magazines. Learn to use the two wonderful reference works you'll find in your public library: the *Readers Guide* (for general magazines) and the *Business Periodical Index* (for business magazines). Articles reaching back as far as twenty years are catalogued by year, title, author, and subject. You are just as likely to find valuable information in a 1947 issue of the *Satur-*

day Evening Post or *Fortune*, or even the *Ladies' Home Journal*, as you are in *Advanced Management* or the *Zinc Smelters Journal*. Your public library will help you find material on any subject you name.

4. Business and Trade Associations

These range from the National Association of Manufacturers and the Chamber of Commerce of the United States to smaller groups concentrating on a particular business, industry, or area. All of them publish material and are usually glad to give it out to members and nonmembers alike. The publications may be full-size magazines like the regularly appearing *Banker* of the American Bankers Association or occasional pamphlets and information sheets. Your local public or university library will probably have some of these in a pamphlet file. Keep your eyes open as you read government publications about your industry: suggesttions about private reading material are given quite frequently. Write to the associations direct and they will flood you with material.

5. "Services"

You're familiar with *Dun and Bradstreet, Moody's,* and *Poor's Manuals* in the financial field. Such services abound in great numbers in other fields, too. Examples are *Public Relations News, Real Estate Analyst, Housing Letter.* To locate the service you need, look in the *Handbook of Commercial and Financial and Information Services,* published by the Special Libraries Association, New York City. It lists and describes 577 separate services. Some of these services are expensive to the subscriber, but they're cheap if they lead to bigger profits or help you avoid costly mistakes.

6. Books

I'm firmly convinced that every businessman worthy of the name should have a business library and consult it frequently. My own shelves contain about a thousand books. Maybe you won't want or need that many, but don't be without at least a limited business library. What I'm trying toget across to you is: *don't* try to run your business without taking advantage of the concentrated knowledge, work, and effort of the thousands of people who have gone before you and who have put that knowledge between the covers of books for *you*. That's like driving your car with two cylinders missing.

BIBLIOGRAPHY

U.S. Department of Commerce, Business and Defense Services Administration. *Marketing Information Guide* (Monthly). $2.00 per year; single copy 15 cents.

U.S. Department of Commerce, Office of Technical Services. Patent Abstract Series.

———. *Technical Reports Newsletter* (Monthly).

———. *U.S. Government Research Reports* (Twice a month). $15.00 per year; single copy $1.00.

U.S. Department of Health, Education, and Welfare, Office of Education. *A Directory of 3,660 16-mm Film Libraries.* $1.00.

U.S. Patent Office. *Official Gazette of the U.S. Patent Office* (Weekly). $35.00 per year.

Small Business Administration. *Federal Handbook for Small Business.*

———. Management Aids Series.

———. *Products List Circular.*

CHAPTER VI

UNCLE SAM AS YOUR
BEST CUSTOMER

SELLING YOUR BIGGEST ACCOUNT

WITH GOVERNMENT HELP

COME ON IN, THE WATER'S FINE!

Have you had the idea that only the industrial giant corporations of this country can do business with the United States Government? Have you felt that you, as a small businessman, didn't have a chance for a federal contract? Well, that's a general feeling among smaller businessmen, and it's absolutely false. The plain fact is that almost any businessman, however small, can have Uncle Sam for a customer, if he really wants to. The government enters into thousands of contracts every year that can easily be handled by small firms. If you're not getting your share of this profitable business, perhaps you should look into it right now.

In most cases small companies shy away from this business because they do not understand the purchasing methods used by the government. They are afraid of the "red tape." So, rather than get bogged down in what they consider complex bidding rules—rather than tackle the paper work—they decide to take a rain check. How wrong they are! Of course there's an amount of paper work involved; of course you have to abide by the rules the government sets down; but once you've taken the trouble to learn the simple procedures required to become one of Uncle Sam's suppliers, almost anyone in your company can handle the details. And when you stop to consider that Uncle can very likely give you *more business* than you're now getting from *all* of your present customers, it's certainly worth the initial effort to get started on this tremendous source of income.

Your "bible" on how to sell to the government is a free book put out by the General Services Administration (Washington 25, D.C.) entitled *Doing Business with the Federal Government*. Reading this book, you'll learn how anxious the government is to cut you in. In framing the Small Business Act, Congress especially directed that small business should receive a fair share of government contracts. The book will give you the how, where, and what of selling to the federal government and will answer most of your questions about the deals you can make.

Once you've read this clearly written, well-illustrated book, a lot of your fears will simply evaporate. You'll be ready to take stock of your own resources and decide what you have to offer that Uncle Sam may need. And he needs plenty! As the country's biggest business firm, the government buys everything from thumbtacks to power plants. This book outlines the basic principles on which the government buys. You're told your responsibilities as a contractor, and you're even given advice on how to buy government-owned property. This extremely informative book of some 90 pages is capped off with facsimiles of most of the standard forms you'll need to know about when doing business with your government.

If you can read only one book on this subject, it should be *Doing Business with the Federal Government*.

In clear, down-to-earth terms, the first part covers competitive bids, quality control, standards, and specifications the government will insist on. It takes up certain special types of contracts which may be of interest to you. It will also refer you to other publications to keep you informed on changes and new items the government is looking for.

The book covers the various government departments, one by one, and gives you some idea of their needs. A few of these will surprise you. Do you sell small boats, fishing nets, or hiking boots? The Bureau of Commercial Fisheries may be looking for them. Do you make or sell anything that a physician, dentist, or hospital might need? Check into the daily want list of the Department of Health, Education, and Welfare. The Agriculture Library buys books and library supplies. The Maritime Administration is on the lookout for paint, rust preventives, and metal-conditioning compounds. And a real bonanza exists in the Bureau of Public Roads if you can supply road-construction equipment and supplies.

All this, of course, only scratches the surface. A much more specific reference work, still from the small businessman's point of view, is the *Purchasing Specifications and Sales Directory* put out by the SBA for 60 cents. After a good deal of actual basic information about selling to the government and to government contractors (subcontracting), it lists in alphabetical order the specific products and services specially needed by both military and civilian purchasing offices. The products range from abrasives to zinc ribbon. There are some 60 pages, covering more than a thousand such products with code numbers following each item to identify the offices desiring that item. Sometimes only one code number follows an item (such as Altar cloths, 506). Sometimes there are twenty or more code numbers, indicating a much wider need for more commonly used items. But following through on Altar cloths (Code 506), for instance, we're in for a surprise. Code No. 506 leads us to all of the Veterans Administration Hospitals, regional offices, and supply depots—a total of more than a hundred markets for this single item!

And the beauty of it is, you have just as much chance of getting this order as the largest firm in the country. The government only insists on getting quality at a price, exactly like your other customers.

GENERAL SERVICES ADMINISTRATION . . .

While we've concentrated on the Small Business Administration as your particular friend, you don't want to ignore another agency of great value. That's the General Services Administration, which, as the name indicates, is a kind of catchall business and supply agency for the *other* agencies of the government. GSA buys, stores, distributes, and maintains government supplies and property; it also does a lot of the transportation, paper work, and records work for executive agencies.

The Children's Bureau of the Department of Health, Education, and Welfare, for instance, may find it easier and cheaper to get its paper clips, wastebaskets, janitor supplies, or whatever from the GSA than to go out and contract for such things on its own. Since literally hundreds of government agencies do the same, this makes GSA a gigantic and very convenient market for you and the manufacturer or distributor of paper clips, wastebaskets, or janitor supplies. Instead of knocking on the doors of a hundred government departments, you sell a hundred times as much to *one* buyer.

And don't be backward about putting in your oar. The GSA, like the SBA, *wants* to do business with the smaller supplier; you'll be received just as cordially as General Motors when you have something to sell. GSA maintains twelve regional offices throughout the country in addition to the Washington headquarters; so you don't have to travel to do your business face to face. These offices will advise you of the locations of contracting offices; tell you how to get on bidders' mailing lists; where and how to get government specifications so that you'll know your product or service will meet the standards. They'll show you how to keep up to the minute on current bidding opportunities; they'll even give you valuable tips on how to introduce new products to government supply systems and how to promote demand and sales of your present products. In short, they'll knock themselves out to tell you what steps to take, what forms to use, and whom to contact when you want to do business with the government, and all this through trained people whose knowledge is at your disposal at no charge or fee.

Like the Small Business Administration, the General Services Administration puts out heaps of printed material specially tailored for the small businessman looking for a government contract. Some recent books available for the asking are:

Doing Business with the Federal Government
Surplus Government Personal Property Sales Information
Disposal of Surplus Real Property
Public Building Design and Construction
Leasing Space to the Government
A Guide to Specification and Standards of the Federal Government

Note that booklet on *Leasing Space to the Government*. The GSA acts as the government's rental agent not only on building and warehouse space but in other fields. For instance: GSA is open for bids on auto-repair contracts and U-Drive rentals at the seventy-five or more motor pools it runs.

Incidentally, you can get a Federal Buying Directory of Washington, D.C., free from the GSA. This is a handy wall-type chart that will help you to identify quickly the various agencies interested in specific products.

One edge the big firm has over the small businessman in competing for government business is know-how. But the GSA does its best to equalize that gap by letting you know exactly what the government expects. A leaflet on *Sales Promotion and Its Importance in Selling to the Federal Government* warns you that you can't simply bid; you've got to merchandise your product just as you would to a private buyer. You've got to satisfy the government that your product or service will do the job economically and efficiently.

It all boils down to one word: *sell*. This goes double when you're introducing a new or improved product or service. The buying official is not going out of his way to sell your product for you; it's up to you to go to the "consumer"—in this case, the agency that's going to use it —and sell *them* on its superiority.

"SELLING TO THE MILITARY" . . .

That's the title of a 25-cent booklet published by the Department of Defense, which is your direct guide and source book in selling to the Army, Navy, Marine Corps, Air Force, and the Joint Agencies.

As you know, the biggest slice of Uncle Sam's budget

dollar goes for defense spending, and most of that slice is funneled right back into the business world. Iron and steel, dynamos and transistors, airplanes and ships, are contracted out to private firms to dig, make, ship, and build. Even where the government handles the work on a do-it-yourself basis, salaries and wages are paid to soldiers and sailors, civil-service engineers and steam fitters, planners and draftsmen. What happens to all that money? Why, they spend it to buy the things you sell, of course! So whether your business is apples or zithers, get in there and cash in on the military dollar.

The Department of Defense wants to do business with *all* competent firms; it *wants* competition to be as wide as possible. Small firms and firms in labor-surplus areas are especially invited to offer their products to supply defense needs.

That word *needs* is the real key. As in any business, to make a go of it you must learn your customer's needs. Then you must find out his buying policies and follow leads to search out selling opportunities. One of the best ways to find the needs of the government is through the *Commerce Business Daily*.

This is a newspaper published every day (Monday through Friday); subscription is $20.00 a year, or $56.00 for the air-mail edition. This daily paper keeps you posted on the very latest information you'll need to sell to both the military and civilian sides of the government. All proposed contract awards of over $10,000 are listed as well as awarded contracts above $25,000. The listing of firms which have received their good-sized contracts is your direct lead for subcontracting opportunities. Most of these firms will want to farm out jobs for parts, sub-assemblies, services, and supplies to someone, and it might as well be you. To get the *Commerce Business Daily*, make your check or money order payable to the U.S. Department of Commerce and mail it to:

U.S. Department of Commerce
Administrative Services Office
433 West Van Buren Street, Room 1300
Chicago 7, Illinois

You'll find it one of the best investments you ever made.

WORLD'S BIGGEST CUSTOMER . . .

The military arm of the government uses supplies not only in great quantity but also in bewildering variety. Glancing through the book, *Selling to the Military*, you expect to see calls for ammunition and generators, explosives and jet planes. But golf clubs? Ant farms? Women's panties? Toy soldiers? Caviar? Insecticides? Absolutely! The Post Exchanges and the Quartermaster Corps need just about everything under the sun. The book lists the principal interests of the Military Exchange Service (the Post Exchange or "PX"), which are candy and confections; beverages; tobacco and accessories; toiletries and drugs; stationery and supplies; clothing and accessories; jewelry, toys, housewares, and accessories; sports and recreational equipment and supplies; automotive accessories; food.

Some time ago, we manufactured plastic Toy Soldiers to retail at $1.00 for a box of one hundred pieces. Naturally, our primary market was the toy stores in the country. But imagine our surprise when sales to PX's soon began to outstrip our sales to toy stores! And not only did the PX's move thousands and thousands of sets for us, but we had no credit losses, for in effect we were selling to the United States Government.

So the next time you think of selling a product to the government, don't necessarily think in terms of guided missiles or electronic equipment running into millions of dollars; instead, think of our selling these little Toy Soldiers by the thousands, and perhaps it will give you a wider view on marketing *your* products to Uncle Sam. So jump right in and get your share of the billions of dollars being spent to make our country strong. If you miss out on this fertile source of business, you're not only hurting yourself but passing up a wonderful chance to help your country.

GOT AN INVENTIVE MIND? . . .

How about putting it to work for Uncle Sam? Believe it or not, he'll buy your inventions and pay you good money for them, provided they're what he wants. And he tells you exactly what he needs in *Inventions Wanted,* a free publication of the Department of Commerce. It lists more than six hundred inventions wanted by the armed forces and other government agencies. Just to give you an idea of the scope of inventions needed, here are a few "wants" listed in the book.

Self-Luminous Paint. This paint must be readily seen in the dark, should require no external excitation, emit no harmful radiation, and maintain its brightness for a minimum of five years. Such a paint is required for safe and adequate illumination of instrument dials, meters, signs, etc.

Heat-Resistant Paint. Heat-resistant paint capable of retaining adhesion, film integrity, and color up to temperatures of 1,000°F for extended (2 or more hours) periods of time. *Present situation and requirements:* Paints such as this are available for service only at temperatures less than 650°F.

Aircraft Paint. An aircraft paint which will resist rain erosion at temperatures beyond 300°F at high Mach numbers.

New Methods of Making Colored Smokes. In present smoke mixtures the dye (40 per cent of the mix) is volatilized by an oxidizing material (60 per cent of the mix). About 80 per cent to 90 per cent of the dye is lost by decomposition. A composition or method which would substantially reduce this loss of dye is desired. A possible solution might be the discovery of a mixture of several dye intermediates which can be caused to react to form the dye and at the same time produce sufficient heat to volatilize the dye without undue decomposition.

Self-Luminous Material. Scope: Luminous sheet material which will glow in the dark without external excitation for marking roadways, buildings, obstructions, personnel, etc. If radioactive, the emitted radiation must be below tolerance level. It is essential that the sheet be fabricated from nontoxic materials. Brightness should be minimum of one "effective microlambert."

Sound-Absorbing Material. A lightweight sound-absorbing material for use in helicopters and jet planes that is far superior to present materials. Perhaps it might combine other functions such as armor plate and insulation.

There are few ways in which you can be of more service to your country—and incidentally, benefit yourself—than by applying your inventive talents to these problems.

RESEARCH AND DEVELOPMENT . . .

Research and development is a new and magic word combination. It can be just as important to you, the small businessman, as it is to Rand or Convair. You're invited to contribute your share in this exciting field and to take advantage of the profitable business opportunities it offers.

The Small Business Act of 1958 ordered government agencies to give all possible help to small business in the activities of government research. In the free booklet, *Small Business Guide to Government Research and Development Opportunities*, you'll find a complete run-down on the contract opportunities open to you. Every department and agency lists its main interests, and you are even told what the individual smaller departments are looking for.

This book contains valuable information on how you can land a big research and/or development contract with the government, and it also refers you to other publications on this subject. You're told how to offer proposals, and any organization or person is free to suggest an idea for research and development. I've been told that amateur cameramen, after studying slow-motion movies made of birds in flight, have come up with the idea of slotted wings for planes—an idea which may revolutionize aviation. As a businessman, you'll think, perhaps, of the type of research connected with your own products. If you are qualified to carry out the research, you'll be favorably considered for the job if the government decides it's worth investigating.

Every business firm interested in getting an R&D contract from the government is asked to prepare a brochure to convince the government that the firm is capable of carrying through the job efficiently and successfully. The valuable booklet we are talking about gives you tips on how to prepare this brochure and what to put in it. Again, remember: this is a *selling job* to convince the technical personnel in the government agency that you can handle the assignment if they award it to you.

Every SBA regional office has a specialist on tap to answer your questions; and there's also a Small Business Specialist at each procuring agency, arsenal, or laboratory who should be contacted first with your ideas. They have your best interests at heart.

THE WILD BLUE ...

Ever think *your* product might land on the moon? It's possible! The National Aeronautics and Space Administration (NASA) is a source of business very much like the military. Send for the free booklet, *Selling to NASA*, which will tell you:

> The supplies and services which NASA buy number in the thousands—from routine office supplies to complex construction projects, from miniature electronic components to large spacecraft sysems. Your business, plant or laboratory might well be an important source of supplies or technical know-how in any of a number of important NASA contracts, no matter how small or "routine" your activities may be.

Like the military, NASA wants ideas. It conducts research and development in the same way, looks for the best-qualified organizations, and urges you, if you have an original idea in NASA's field, to submit it without waiting to be asked.

As for products, NASA spends 75 per cent of its funds with private industry and business, along with educational and research organizations. And NASA is going to keep right on spending that way.

It's up to you to get yourself on NASA's bidding list, explaining in detail what you can offer. The purchasing office sends out bidding invitations to the list of suppliers of the items or services it wants. Write to NASA headquarters in Washington, D.C., for the forms you'll have to fill out to get on the list.

For subcontracting, you apply directly to NASA's prime contractors. A Small Business Adviser at NASA headquarters or in any of the centers of NASA activity will give you a list of the prime contractors. He'll also help you in any other way possible. Write to:

NASA Directory
NASA Headquarters
National Aeronautics and Space Administration
Washington 25, D.C.

So get started today looking into the opportunities in NASA. The sky's the limit!

BUYING FROM THE GOVERNMENT . . .

When I headed this chapter "Uncle Sam as Your Best Customer," I'm afraid I was holding back on you. Oh, the heading is true; it just doesn't go quite far enough. You see, Uncle Sam wants to sell *to* you as well as buy *from* you. He has a tremendous amount of both land and merchandise, and he offers most of it at bargains you've got to see to believe. So, just as he can be your best customer, he can, in certain cases, be your biggest source of supply at fantastically low prices. Let's look into this big plus right now.

A LAND-OFFICE BUSINESS . . .

That's what the government is running, all the time. Vast areas of land are continually being put up for sale. You may have to get in line behind public agencies— states, civic organizations, and other nonprofit agencies— which are given first refusal and healthy discounts, especially on lands they plan to use for public health, education, recreation, or wildlife conservation. But all other surplus real estate of the government is usually offered for sale through advertising on a competitive-bidding basis.

For a quick run-down on the details and variety of these opportunities, write to General Services Administration for a free leaflet entitled *Disposal of Surplus Real Property*. And to learn of particular sales, with descriptions of the property scheduled to be sold, write the Department of Commerce; get yourself put on its mailing list for the daily *Synopsis of U.S. Government Proposed Procurement, Sales and Contract Awards*. These are listed by region, in case you're interested in a particular part of the country.

HOMESTEADS . . .

Homestead land is land the government will give you free if you agree to improve it. A hundred years ago it was possible for a settler to stake out over 500 acres of land, through farming, timber, and grazing tracts. This was the government's way of encouraging our hardy grandfathers to come out and build up the West.

Nowadays, however, there's little agricultural public land left, and the rules have changed. But you can still homestead five acres, sometimes more. If you're lucky you may find a piece you can use for a mountain, desert, or river cabin. You have to build on it within a specified period of time, whereupon it becomes yours. The government charges you nothing, but you may have to pay nominal registering, surveying, and perhaps county charges. Almost all the public-domain land left is either in Alaska or west of the Rockies. Much of it is desert or mountain, and all the rest is leased out for grazing, timber, or mining. For information, write to the Department of the Interior, Bureau of Land Management, Washington, D. C.

SMALL TRACTS . . .

Few people know about an attractive opportunity in land through the Small Tract Act of 1938. Any citizen may obtain a tract up to five acres on which to live, play, or establish a business. These lands are not free; some desirable tracts have sold for several thousand dollars. Such expensive tracts may be on a main road or just outside the border of a national park and in a very desirable place to put up a café, motel, or filling station. But it's safe to say that whatever you pay for the tract, it will still be a bargain.

All the information you'll need to put you next to this opportunity can be found in a free booklet, *Small Tracts*, put out by the Bureau of Land Management. Instead of buying the tract outright, you may lease it or lease with the right to purchase at a fixed price after two or three years. During that period you must put up improvements (such as a house), as the Bureau of Land Management directs. You can readily see how a tract in a well-chosen location, with the improvements, may be worth much more than the sale price by the time your option is up. Many enterprising businessmen have made a good deal out of this opportunity Uncle Sam offers.

OTHER GOVERNMENT REAL ESTATE . . .

If you're prospecting for minerals, you're welcome to stake a claim in the time-honored way on public-domain land, including national-forest lands. After complying with the mining laws, you can secure title to the land through a "patent" (meaning "ownership papers," not to be confused with the "invention" kind of patent). Keep in mind, however, that you must have discovered minerals on the claimed spot. If you want to know the procedure for this, ask the Bureau of Land Management for a copy of *Circular No. 1278*—no charge.

If you want to irrigate, cultivate, and improve desert land, you can get it for $1.25 an acre in the western states. Unfortunately, most of the tracts with the best water sources were grabbed up long ago. You'll have to satisfy the government that you own the water rights and have a plan to irrigate and pay for the land.

Certain deposits of oil, gas, coal, potash, sodium, and phosphates in government lands can be leased or bought. The local land office of the area you're interested in will refer you to the proper source for these deals. In some cases, don't be surprised if you end up doing business with an Indian tribe!

If you are interested in quarrying sand, gravel, or

building stone on government lands, you can make arrangements to buy or lease with the Bureau of Land Management or the Forest Service. The same applies to timber and forest products.

Also, grazing rights can be had on federal lands, including the national forests. See the Bureau of Land Management.

And finally, to round out the real-estate picture, you can buy an old fort, a lighthouse, or an island, if such is your wish. General Services Administration inherited real estate to the tune of 9 billion dollars after the end of World War II. Most of this has been disposed of to communities, but there's still a lot of it left. Ask the GSA for listings, which keep changing as more and more of the parcels are put on the market. Many buildings left over from Army camps are still valuable. The GSA sells them usually through sealed bids, but small business gets the edge if the bids are reasonably close. In this type of deal, small business is defined as a concern with fewer than five hundred employees. And you can buy on credit, too. Write to the nearest regional office of the GSA for more information about this.

SURPLUS, IT'S WONDERFUL . . .

Besides real property, the government wants to sell you, at bargain prices, literally mountains of merchandise no longer needed by the agencies which bought it originally. This surplus is not always secondhand merchandise; much of it has never been used. You may find items you can use in your own business, or you may join the many hundreds of traders who buy and sell surplus as a regular business. Since many smaller items are sold in "lots" containing anywhere from a dozen pieces up and since much of the stuff is in its original unopened cases, there's a treasure-hunting element here that appeals to many. Bidding on a lot for a few items in it, you many find something you never realized you bought, which is worth more than you paid for the whole lot.

TO SUM UP . . .

I hope I've convinced you that no matter what your business, it pays you to look into the almost limitless opportunities of doing *some* of your business with Uncle Sam. Through all his agencies for buying and selling, he goes out of his way to favor *you*, the small businessman. You don't have to be big enough to send your salesmen or representatives to the Capital. The government is so eager to buy from you and to sell to you that it practically *comes to you* through the many regional offices of SBA, GSA, and the other agencies.

At the same time, you'll do better for yourself and get the jump on your competition by learning all you can through the books mentioned in this chapter and by making use of the business-service specialists in the government regional offices. Then get your name on the right "bid lists" . . . and good luck!

BIBLIOGRAPHY

General Services Administration (Washington 25, D.C.). *Disposal of Surplus Real Property.* Free.
———. *Doing Business with the Federal Government.* Free.
———. *Leasing Space to the Government.* Free.
———. *Public Building Design and Construction.* Free.

———. *Sales Promotion and Its Importance in Selling to the Federal Government.* Free.

———. *Surplus Government Personal Property Sales Information.* Free.

National Aeronautics and Space Administration (Washington, D.C.). *Selling to NASA.* Free.

National Inventors Council (U.S. Department of Commerce, Washington 25, D.C.). *Inventions Wanted by the Armed Forces and Other Government Agencies*

Small Business Administration (Washington 25, D.C.). *Government Research and Development Opportunities.*

———. *Small Business Guide to Government Research and Development Opportunities.* Free.

———. *U.S. Government Purchasing Specifications and Sales Directory.* 60 cents.

U.S. Department of Commerce. *Commerce Business Daily.* $20.00 per year; $56.00 per year for air-mail edition.

U.S. Department of the Interior, Bureau of Land Management. *Circular No. 1278.* Free.

———. *Small Tracts.* Free.

Superintendent of Documents (Washington, D.C. 20402). *Federal Handbook for Small Business.* Free.

———. *Selling to the Military.* 25 cents.

CHAPTER VII

UNCLE SAM AS YOUR BOSS

A Lifetime Job Working
for the Government

I can just hear you screaming.

"*Me*, work for the government? Me, take a job? I'm a *businessman!*"

All right, simmer down. Look at it this way. Suppose I offered you a $100,000 loan, interest-free, put into escrow as your capital investment to go into business. Interested? You can't touch the capital, but suppose I guarantee you 7, 8, or possibly 10 per cent net profit every year on that investment. (You'll have to pay income taxes on it, of course. I'm no magician!)

Not only that, I promise you'll have no payroll to meet, no bills for goods you wonder if you're able to sell, no sales, excise, or social-security taxes to account for, no personnel problems (except yourself), none of those headaches to worry about which you've been reading of in the chapters up to this one—like ratios, advertising, sales territories. Did I mention that you'll work a forty-hour week and will be able to spend evenings and week ends with your family?

But I'm not through yet. Maybe I should have my head examined, but I'll make my offer still more attractive. In case you fail, quit, go bankrupt, or just decide to walk off and leave the business, I'll tear up your I O U, and we're quits.

What is this, a businessman's dream of heaven? Maybe so; but it's also a pretty good description of a government civil-service job. Actually . . .

THERE'S MONEY IN WORKING FOR THE GOVERNMENT! . . .

Not to mention security, sick leave, overtime and vacation time, regular salary increases, opportunity for promotion, valuable training on the job, and generous retirement pay after you've put in your service.

In fact, if you look on government service as a *business*, it stacks up as a pretty darned attractive one. Many a businessman working all hours, worrying himself into ulcers and an early grave, has less to show at the end of the year than the federal employee with the same training, experience, and ability.

What do government jobs pay? It's true that if you are an electronics engineer or an attorney, you can probably make more in private industry or private practice than in government service. The top civil-service salary at this moment is around $18,500 per year. On the other hand, if you only have more routine abilities, the government service will pay at least as much as and possibly more than you could get in the employ of an outside firm. The average civil-service salary is about $8,000 a year; and that's 8 per cent on a capital of $100,000!

Incidentally, we'll concentrate on civil service in this chapter. There are "excepted" positions, chiefly in the executive branch of the government. They're "excepted" usually because they're of a confidential or policy-level nature. Certain other jobs (such as ambassadorships) are traditionally of a patronage nature; that is, they're appointed without examination. And the Armed Services have certain civilian jobs which they fill without civil-service procedure.

If you can get one, go to it! But these exceptions aside, you'll have to go through the civil-service mill to get your job, whether ditchdigger or federal prosecuting attorney. Your salary will be rated according to a GS

GENERAL SCHEDULE (GS)

Grade	Entrance Salary	Periodic Increase	Maximum Salary
1	$ 3,185	$105	$ 3,815
2	3,500	105	4,130
3	3,760	105	4,390
4	4,040	105	4,670
5	4,345	165	5,335
6	4,830	165	5,820
7	5,355	165	6,345
8	5,885	165	6,875
9	6,435	165	7,425
10	6,995	165	7,985
11	7,560	260	8,860
12	8,955	260	10,255
13	10,635	260	11,935
14	12,210	260	13,510
15	13,730	325	15,030
16	15,255	260	16,295
17	16,530	260	17,570
18	18,500	....	18,500

Don't forget the fringe benefits that make these jobs even more attractive: generous vacations, retirement credit, accumulated sick leave, overtime pay (usually at time and a half).

number. That means General Schedule. The numbers go from 1 to 18; positions are rated according to difficulty. A GS-3 typist, for instance, will normally be expected to handle more difficult work than a GS-2 typist. Incidentally, to give you an idea of salaries, stenotypists can go as high as GS-7 and earn up to $6,345 per year.

See the above schedule.

You go up through the grades by promotional examinations, which are held periodically as needed. Furthermore, the government is a big organization, and it covers a big country. You can frequently get transfers into more congenial types of employment or to other localities without leaving your job or endangering your accumulated benefits.

WHAT KIND OF JOB? . . .

Almost all types of occupations found in private industry are also found in the Federal Civil Service. Chances are, whatever your talent, the government has a need for it and is ready to pay you for it. It would be impossible, almost, to list the bewildering variety of civil-service positions. Here are a few at random.

Accountant	Dentist
Apprentice	Draftsman
Athletic Director	Economist
Attorney	Editor
Bank Examiner	Elevator Operator
Budget Examiner	Farmer
Business Machine Operator	Forester
Carpenter	Geologist
Chemist	Guard
Clerk	Home Economist
Correctional Officer	Inspector

Insurance Officer
Internal Revenue Agent
Investigator
Jobs Overseas
Laborer
Librarian
Mechanic
Metallurgist
Nurse
Occupational Therapist
Pharmacist
Photographer
Physical Therapist

Physician
Physicist
Post Office Clerk
Printer
Proofreader
Psychologist
Purchasing Agent
Social Worker
Statistician
Student Dietitian
Teacher
Veterinarian
Writer

Note how your business experience could make you a natural for such positions as purchasing agent, bank examiner, or any number of other jobs.

Incidentally, don't hang onto the outmoded idea that the government worker is a shovel-leaner, just putting in the time until he draws his retirement pay. If you get a job with Uncle Sam, not only will you be fully qualified (more about the examinations soon), but you'll put in a full day's work for a day's pay.

Under civil service you have over two million jobs to choose from. Your politics don't count; you don't have to know a congressman or pay a commission to get a position. Visit or write the nearest Civil Service Regional Office and ask to be put on the list for jobs available in your categories. Post offices, as well as most public libraries and public buildings, keep the most recent bulletins posted.

When you're interested in a particular position, read the bulletin carefully. If you don't qualify and no exceptions are indicated, forget that job. The bulletin means exactly what it says, including age limits, height and weight (on some jobs), and particularly education and experience. If you *really* want the job and seem to be missing out by a small detail, get in touch with the Civil Service Regional Office and see if they'll accept your application anyway.

Having applied, you'll be given a written and possibly an oral examination. For some jobs, you may also take a practical test. If you pass, you'll be notified of your position on the eligible list. When your turn comes up, you'll be offered the job. It's true that the employing officer has his pick of the three highest-ranking applicants for the job, and he may not like the way you part your hair. On the other hand, you have the privilege of turning down three offers before you're removed from the list.

HOW ABOUT THAT EXAMINATION? . . .

Take it seriously, but don't be afraid of it. If you qualify for the job you're after, if you know the field, you'll find the written examination tough but fair. Go back to that job bulletin. It tells you *exactly* what will be covered in the examination; no more, no less.

Now, what about the content of the examination? What are the questions like? Obviously, the material will vary from job to job. There will be some basic questions, usually, designed to test your general understanding of the meanings of words, of written paragraphs, of simple mathematics, and the like. The Civil Service Commission puts out a number of pamphlets. In this series, No. 11 gives *Specimen Questions from Civil Service Examinations*. The regional office or the U.S. Civil Service Commission in Washington will send it to you on request. When you receive it, look over the sample questions. They'll give you an idea of what you'll be up against.

For particular jobs, the questions cover the areas you'd be expected to know in order to hold down the job. To repeat, the examination is nothing to be afraid of if you really qualify for the position and if you've boned up where necessary on the job material, the laws and regulations governing the job, and whatever is described on the bulletin as part of the examination.

THE ORAL INTERVIEW . . .

In all but the most routine positions, a lot of weight is put on the oral interview. Questions will be asked you by a representative of the Civil Service Commission and the supervisor of the department in which you'll work if you get the job. This is nothing more than an employment interview. It, too, is nothing to be afraid of if you know your stuff. The interviewers will assess your personal characteristics, the things they couldn't get from your written test, such as your general appearance and your ability to express yourself and to get along with people. They may give you what looks like a hard time in trying to see how you conduct yourself under fire, how you think on your feet. This interview is generally used for positions in which you'll have to deal with people and in certain higher-paid jobs.

PHYSICAL EXAMINATION . . .

If you're applying for a job that requires physical stamina, such as mail-sack handler or forester, you'll be required to take a physical examination which is conducted by a medical officer after you've passed the written test and have had your interview and before you're appointed to the job. The physical examination is, of course, for your own benefit as well as the government's. If you have any doubts about passing it, get yourself checked over by your own physician first.

PLUSES AND MINUSES . . .

Any special skill, ability, or aptitude, such as knowledge of foreign languages, accounting, bookkeeping, or typing, is important in putting you ahead of less qualified competitors on the list. The same goes for education beyond the requirements of the application, particularly if it's education that bears on the job.

Veterans

A veteran gets a decided edge in all government employment. If you had wartime or peacetime military service, you get five free points on your written examination. If you're disabled, it goes up to ten points. Send for Pamphlet 12, *Veteran Preference in Federal Employment,* to learn more about these breaks, which include preference in case of staff reduction, too.

Speaking of handicaps, we quote:

Each year several thousand persons with serious, permanent physical handicaps take their place in the Government's career civil service through the selective-placement program of the U.S. Civil Service Commission. Since 1942, more than 137,000 disabled workers have joined Uncle Sam's civilian work force.

The Commission-sponsored Governmentwide program assures the handicapped of consideration for gainful employment. Yet it operates within the framework of the civil-service merit system, providing the disabled equal opportunity for Federal employment but not special preference over other applicants. Not only must the physically handicapped be qualified to do particular jobs, they must also *compete* with nondisabled applicants for such civil-service positions. In the light of this requirement, the success of the selective-placement program emphasizes the truth that *properly placed*, the disabled worker is as good as the nondisabled.

Selective placement emphasizes abilities—not disabilities. It is founded on the principle that the physically handicapped person who is placed in the right position is not handicapped on the job. When it certifies a disabled person to an agency for consideration for employment, the Civil Service Commission is expressing its belief that the person is well qualified to do the full job.

On the other side of the ledger, you cannot get a government job unless you are a citizen; but whether native-born or naturalized makes no difference. If you've had a prior criminal conviction, you may be disqualified, or you may be temporarily barred for two years from a civil-service job. You'll be fingerprinted if appointed, so it doesn't pay to try to hide such a conviction; however, the government policy is to be quite lenient wherever possible, so don't let a past record keep you from trying for the federal service.

The government demands absolute loyalty of its employees, and the tendency has been to tighten up on Communist, Fascist, or other subversive connections.

You and your wife may both work for the government, but the law forbids appointment of any person if *two* or more members of his immediate family, living under the same roof, are employed by the government. This curious requirement is waived, however, if you're a veteran.

There are other obstacles that can keep you out of the civil service. However, they're the same ones you'd run into in applying for a job anywhere: physical or mental unfitness, false statements on the application, cheating on the examination.

You are *not* required to submit a photograph with your application, and you are never asked about race, color, religion, or political affiliation.

Once you start working for the government, you'll find certain of your rights restricted. You don't have the right to strike, although you can join a union or employees' organization, and there are a number of these, usually divided by crafts, such as the National Federation of Post Office Clerks and the National Association of Letter Carriers.

Your right to engage in political activity is rather sharply curbed. Under the Hatch Act, a federal employee cannot actively work for a political party or candidate; he can vote and sign petitions, and that's just about it.

Incidentally, the general impression is that once he's appointed, it takes dynamite to blast a federal employee out of his job. This is not so. As a matter of fact, I believe it's a little *easier* to fire a government worker who misbehaves than a worker in private employment who is protected by a strong union.

WANT A JOB OVERSEAS? . . .

Uncle has plenty of them: room for a quarter of a million American workers in almost every country in the world. What a chance to see the globe and get paid for it! Again, most of these jobs are civil-service, so you get the information in the usual places. In fact, one of the best ways to get an overseas job is to take a job with an agency of the government in the United States. Most overseas jobs are filled by transferred career employees.

DON'T FORGET . . .

Your state, county, and city also employ workers to carry out the functions of their governments. Most of these have civil-service setups modeled more or less after the federal system. Sometimes state and local salary lists run higher than the federal pay for the same jobs, too. So, if you want to earn your "profit" on that $100,000 "capital" I offered you at the beginning of this chapter, look into these job opportunities. Most public buildings, courthouses, and libraries kep the current job-opening bulletins on file, or you may write to your state capital, county seat, or city hall for information. Address your letter to the Personnel Board of these agencies.

A FINAL PLUS . . .

Something I've hesitated to mention up to now is the satisfaction of *service*. I realize that most federal workers look on their jobs as routine with the pay check their only goal. But a lot of people are working for the government who could step out and make much more in private industry or private practice. A prime example is the 20,000 or so young people working for the Peace Corps. They make about 11 cents an hour, but they take the sacrifice willingly because they believe they're helping to create a better world. The same applies to top men—scientists, lawyers, businessmen—who could make ten to fifty times their government salaries in the outside world.

In a less idealistic way, I look at the mountains of

aid the government heaps on its citizens (you've been reading about a small part of it in this book), and I feel that anyone who contributes to this work deserves our thanks and respect.

BIBLIOGRAPHY

U.S. Civil Service Commission Pamphlets.
No. 4. *Working for the U.S.A.*
No. 2. *Basic Acts, Rules and Regulations Governing Employment in the Federal Civil Service*
No. 12. *Veteran Preference in Federal Employment*
No. 16. *Untapped Manpower (Selective Placement of the Physically Handicapped)*
No. 18. *Your Retirement System*
No. 20. *Political Activity of Federal Officers and Employees*
No. 11. *Specimen Questions from Civil Service Examinations*
No. 22H. *The Federal Career Service . . . At Your Service*
No. 25H. *Summer Employment in Federal Agencies*
No. 26H. *The Way to a Job in Government*

CHAPTER VIII

UNCLE SAM AS YOUR PROTECTOR

Safeguarding Your Business

with Government Help

A prominent New York jeweler had a $50,000 diamond and ruby necklace to ship to a customer in Chicago. How did he send it? By special bonded messenger? Not on your life. He wrapped the package in plain brown paper, used his own name and home address for the return address, put on a few stamps, and sent it by *perfectly ordinary parcel post*. He insured it for ten dollars, the way Aunt Mary insures the cookies she sends you for Christmas. And like Aunt Mary's cookies, the package got where it was going. That's Uncle Sam's mail carriers for you. They not only deliver the mail; they deliver it *safely*.

Actually, if your mail gets lost, it's probably your own fault. Address your envelope or parcel correctly and clearly, make sure your return address is also on it, and you can drop it into that familiar red, white, and blue box on the corner and relax. Even with poor addressing, inadequate postage, and badly wrapped packages, the chance of your mail getting lost is less than one in 100,000. You can reduce that chance by keeping mailing lists up to date and by notifying the post office of your own changes of address. You know that even if your customer lives on a country road or fifty miles up the river, Uncle Sam will see—somehow—that he gets the mail you send him.

That's why I say a little prayer of thanks every night for the United States Post Office, and so should you. I don't care what business you're in; you'd have a lot rougher time of it without the mails. Even letters burned in a plane wreck have turned up at my office after going through the hands of the famed "nixie" clerks: those wizards who can make sense out of just about anything.

In my previous book, I said that while the postage stamp is your greatest sales tool, you must bear in mind that it carries a heavy obligation to be scrupulously honest at all times, for Uncle Sam protects the *content* of the mail as well as the mail itself. Through his post-office inspectors, he is working night and day to stop racketeers from stealing your money. As a matter of fact, the inspectors spend more than a quarter of their time running down and halting mail frauds. Besides this, they keep the mails clear of obscene and threatening letters, lotteries, firearms, explosives, and poisons. They're known as such tough lads where criminal statutes are broken that "con" artists will go to great lengths to avoid sending or receiving letters in the course of their crooked business.

A few months back my wife fell for a phony pitch in a newspaper ad. She sent money for a promotional book of "free" neighborhood services, which turned out to be anything but free. I called up the sender and tried to get her money back. He was giving me a hard time, until I casually mentioned that I'd take the matter up with the postal inspectors. I got a check back the next day.

All this is mighty important to you as a businessman.

It means that your legitimate business by mail is received with confidence—a confidence backed up by Uncle Sam. He spends millions to keep up the reputation of the mails, and you reap the benefit.

At the same time, it's easy to overstep the rules without really intending to, so I suggest you pick up a *Postal Guide* on your next trip to the post office, read it, and learn the regulations you're expected to follow.

As a businessman, you'll be interested in knowing that when you stamp that letter, you're dealing with the nation's biggest business—actually one of the biggest in the world. The Postmaster-General, the head man in charge of all postal activity, operates 45,000 post offices and employs 600,000 workers with a payroll of $10,500,000 a *day*. He has a fleet of 50,000 government-owned cars and trucks and leases another 50,000. Right now, he's going into automation in a big way to help move the mountains of mail you and I and our fellow businessmen pour on him every day.

UNCLE SAVES YOUR MONEY . . .

He saves and protects your money in any number of ways. Let's start with the post office. Although higher interest in other investments has cut into it somewhat, Postal Savings is still the only way thousands of persons save. Their nearest post office is their bank; they accept the low 2 per cent interest rate, knowing that their money is as secure as the government itself.

Probably the most popular direct savings plan offered by the government is, of course, the U.S. Savings Bonds program. E and H bonds are about the safest savings you can find. You buy E bonds at 75 per cent of their maturity value: that is, a $100 bond costs you $75. But if you

hold it for the full 7 years 9 months, you can cash it for
$100. However, the bond is cashable at any time at any
bank. It's value at any period short of maturity is printed
right on the bond itself. Your interest is 4¼ per cent for
the bond held the full time; somewhat less if you cash
it in earlier. Thus you get a bonus for holding the bond
the full period.

The H bonds come in denominations of $500 to
$10,000 and mature in 10 years. On these you pay the face
value and your interest is 4¼ per cent if held to maturity
for the full ten-year period. The interest is paid directly to
you by check every six months after the first six months.
by check every six months.

Both E and H bonds are universally sold through
banks, savings and loan associations, and payroll-deduc-
tion plans of employers.

Uncle Sam protects your money in other ways than
just socking it in his bank. For instance, you don't have
to bite every coin to make sure it's genuine. The Secret
Service fights counterfeiters around the clock for you
and keeps your danger of loss through this crime down
to a minimum.

On the other hand, through the Federal Reserve
and other agencies, the government preserves the value
of your good dollar. It's true that inflation has been
eating into it for some time and will probably keep on
eating. But the United States dollar is still just about the
soundest currency in the world, thanks to Uncle's unceas-
ing efforts to keep it so.

Uncle Sam also protects you when you put your
savings into a bank or a savings and loan association. The
Federal Deposit Insurance Corporation guarantees your
deposit to the tune of $15,000. If you're old enough to
remember the time—before 1933—when banks popped

like firecrackers all over the land, you will realize the wonderful work this government agency has done in protecting your savings dollar.

In addition, Uncle Sam protects your business dollar through the Federal Trade Commission. This agency stops unfair business practices, interference with normal business competition, and crooked or lying sharpers who prey on other businessmen and the public. Thanks to the FTC, your gold ring marked "14-k" actually contains fourteen-carat gold, and your "100 per cent wool" sweater is exactly that. The FTC stops price-fixing conspiracies and August fur sales that run all year round. The Commission is glad to hear details on possible frauds or misrepresentation. The action they take may not get your money back, but it will clean up the business atmosphere for future dealings. Incidentally, they'll keep your information confidential. The address is Washington 25, D.C.

When you speculate on the stock market or invest your money in stock, as some thirty million Americans do, your funds are protected from sharp practices by the watchful agents of the Securities and Exchange Commission. They keep a file on every new stock and bond issue offered for public sale, making sure that all important facts are available to you in making your choice. The commission watches for abuses that would cheat you of a fair shake in the market; however, it does *not* approve, disapprove, or advise you on any stock or bond issue. Where you risk your money is your own affair, but you have the comfort of knowing that the information on the prospectus is complete and accurate.

Recently, the Federal Reserve Board raised stock margins to 70 per cent from 50 per cent. Instead of putting up $5,000 to buy $10,000 in stocks, a buyer has to put up $7,000. Margin requirements are changed from time to time, depending on the amount of speculation on credit and the state of the market.

Your freedom to compete fairly with other businesses is protected through federal antitrust laws and is constantly watched over by the Anti-Trust Division of the Department of Justice. Older businessmen will remember the days when business was a jungle in which the big and powerful swallowed up the small and weak. All this was changed by the Clayton and Sherman antitrust laws.

If you're in agriculture, shipping, or the merry-go-round business, to name just a few, you know how your business life depends on the weather. The United States Weather Bureau scientists can't deliver rain or shine, hot or cold weather, to your order (although they're working on it!), but they can do the next best thing by warning you of storms, rain, or fine weather, so you'll know whether to stock ice cream or hot soup in your restaurant, whether to plan on that business trip now or hold off until next week.

People joke about weather forecasts, but farmers trust them. Crop producers have learned that crops grow only during days when the temperature reaches a certain level. By adding "grow" days and subtracting "non-grow" days on the forecast, they save thousands in planning for harvest and shipping.

For daily weather information, your best bet is your local radio, newspaper, or (in some cities) telephone service. The bureau puts out a five-day forecast twice a week. You can also order the *Daily Weather Map* ($7.20 a year) and the *Monthly Weather Outlook* ($4.80 a year) from the Superintendent of Documents.

UNCLE SAM PROTECTS YOUR PRODUCTS . . .

You don't have to be a farmer to be interested in the safety of meat, milk, or poultry. The Department of Agriculture inspects animals, grades meat and poultry, and keeps a weather eye out to see that processed products, such as sausage and cheese, are not only safe to eat but meet standards so that you get what you pay for and not something inferior or cheaper.

Here's an article I found in today's newspaper.

> ANY RESIDUES OF CHLORDANE IN FOOD BANNED (Washington) (AP). The Food and Drug Administration announced Monday it proposes to bar from interstate commerce food crops bearing any residues of the pesticide chlordane. Tolerances for residues of 0.3 part in a million of chlordane are now in effect for 47 fruit and vegetable crops. These were established in 1955, based on 1950 toxicity studies.

The Department of Health, Education, and Welfare—the newest department of the President's Cabinet—has taken over responsibility for the Pure Food and Drug Laws, as well as the Public Health Service. Through the efforts of this department, you can read on the label exactly what any package contains, plus its correct weight or volume. Dangerous cosmetics, once very common, are now controlled. And of course the Narcotics Bureau works full time to stamp out the traffic in habit-forming drugs.

PROTECTION AND MORE PROTECTION . . .

Run down the listings in your phone directory under "United States Government." You'll be surprised at how many agencies are protecting your health, your safety, your children, your old age, your widow.

Beginning with the obvious benefits of protection you get from the Army, Air Force, Navy, Marine Corps, the FBI, and the agencies we've already mentioned, the list is long. The Federal Housing Administration protects your home by insisting on certain building standards before granting a mortgage loan. The low down payment and fair terms of FHA loans has brought home-ownership within the reach of millions who formerly couldn't dream of it.

The Interstate Commerce Commission's Bureau of Safety and Service is on the job to make rail and highway travel safer for you.

In the air, you're safer because the Civil Aeronautics Bureau is in there pitching to prevent accidents. Every air crash is gone over carefully to discover the cause and to correct matters if humanly possible. One of the earliest CAB cases involved a crash that nobody could figure out until an inspector noticed that a thermos bottle had rolled into the "boot" or floor depression at the base of the joystick and had jammed the stick. No matter how hard he pulled, the aviator (they didn't call 'em pilots then) couldn't lift the plane out of a fatal dive. The CAB spread the word. Fliers covered the boot in their planes even before a law could be passed requiring it. The CAB authorities can only estimate how many lives were saved through this action alone.

Ever stop to think of the breaks you get from that ogre, the Director of Internal Revenue, because you're a businessman? Maybe you see red at the mention of taxes. Don't let this blind you to the fact that if your income came entirely from wages, you'd be considerably worse off. You'd have no travel, entertainment, or other business-expense deductions, no fast depreciation write-off of your plant and equipment, no advantages to gain through leasing your car and other perfectly legal tax savings. Capital gains would be a word rather than money in your pocket; the same goes for the lush 27½ per cent allowances if you happen to be in oil or one of the other "depletion" commodities.

No question about it; as a businessman, you're Uncle's favorite nephew!

GOT ANY IDEAS? . . .

For a new "article, composition of matter, apparatus or process?" If so, run—don't walk—to the United States Patent Office. There you'll join your sixty million or so fellow citizens who every year take out a patent.

We talked in Chapter V about how you might profit by someone else's patent. Here, I'd like to give you a brief run-down on how to protect your own valuable ideas through following a few basic steps.

1. Make sure your idea is practical. Don't waste money and time, as many do, trying to patent inventions that have no earthly use. The Patent Office urges you—and I do, too—to ask yourself first, will people need this? Use it? Pay for it? If the answer is no, forget it.

2. Get witnesses to verify the date you first thought up the idea. If you have a drawing, get a trusted friend

to sign and date it. You may not be the only one working on this idea. But if you have the date witnessed, if you keep good records of progress, you may win out in a later dispute. (Incidentally, don't count on a registered letter you mail to yourself. This won't protect you. As a matter of fact, even the witnesses are not *protection*, only evidence. Your invention is fully protected only when it's patented.)

3. Run a search before you plunge. Your idea may not be as new as you think. You can make the search yourself in Washington or at one of the repository libraries in most large cities. Ask your public library to tell you where the nearest one is. However, the Patent Office advises hiring an expert. The Patent Office will send you a list of registered "practitioners," either in Washington (this costs $1.00) or in your own region (free).

After you've studied the patents which are close to your own idea, you've got to make up your own mind about going ahead. This is a business decision. If your idea is essentially better than the others, more practical and more salable, then go ahead. Remember, you cannot cover old features even with a new use. For instance, you can't patent the wheel even if it is a part of your own invention.

Once you decide to go ahead, you'll need an attorney or agent to help you prepare the application. He'll know how to describe your invention, how to push claims for its novelty; he'll know the technical problems and pitfalls. He'll save you a possible rejection. When you get it, the patent is yours for 17 years and may be renewed for another 17 years.

After you obtain your patent, it's up to you to make

it a commercial success. For $3.00 the Patent Office will publish a notice on your patent in the *Official Gazette* letting the world know it's available for sale or lease. The Small Business Administration, the guardian angel of the small businessman, will give you lots of helpful advice and information about locating possible buyers and users of your patent.

WANNA WRITE A BOOK? . . .

Just as Uncle Sam protects your invention from theft and misuse with patenting, he'll protect your written material with a copyright. Under the copyright law, a "book" may be anything from a two-line verse to a twenty-volume encyclopedia. It may be anything written, drawn, photographed, printed, or mapped, including movies, musical compositions, lectures, sermons ,and speeches, models and designs for works of art.

Unlike getting a patent, which is a long-drawn-out, difficult and expensive job, a copyright can be had without expert help for a few dollars. It gives you the right to publish, sell, reprint, or translate your work into other languages. Anyone who uses your material without your permission is in serious legal trouble.

To get a copyright, wait until your work is in print, then send two copies of the best edition to the Register of Copyrights, Library of Congress, Washington, D.C. The Register will issue you application blanks on request, free. The book must bear the copyright imprint, "Copyright, 19....., by [author's or publisher's name]." This must be printed on the title page or the page following it. The two copies will be placed in the Library of Congress.

Your copyright will be good for 28 years, and in the final year it may be renewed for another 28 years by yourself or your heirs. It may be renewed only once, however. If you fail to renew, and after the 56 years at any rate, the work falls into the "public domain" and may be used by anyone.

Many writers, among them Mark Twain, have fought long and bitterly against this provision. They argued that after 56 years, even though most books are worthless to their authors anyway, the rare exceptions should continue to benefit the author or his heirs. But Uncle Sam is not likely to relax on this matter.

Although the United States is not a member of the International Copyright Union, we do have agreements with many other countries to respect each other's copyrights. For more information, write to the Register of Copyrights, Washington, D.C., for a copy of *Copyright Office of the U.S.A.* It's free.

KODAK, FRIGIDAIRE, COKE . . .

We use these words as part of our language, but actually they are registered trade-marks. If you don't believe it, just try to put out a new camera and call it a Kodak. Eastman Kodak Company will come down on you like a landslide. The firm probably carries the value of that little word on its books at a million dollars.

The history of trade-marks goes way back to the days when your medieval ancestor knew he could get the best pint of beer at the Sign of the Gilded Boar, or something of the sort. He could turn over a piece of fine china and see the mark of the maker on the back which was the symbol of the maker's pride, reputation, and responsibility for his product.

The government protects your trade-mark from misuse in the same way it protects your inventions and your writings. You register it through the Patent Office. You have to conduct the same kind of search to make sure you're not accidentally stepping on someone else's toes. You can do this yourself at the Patent Office or at one of the repository libraries; and you can probably draw up your own application, which is much simpler than a patent application.

Before you can register it, the trade-mark must have been in use. If you're in a hurry with a new product, just send a free sample to a friend in another state. That makes it "interstate commerce" and meets the law.

The filing fee is $15.00, which you send in with the written application (get this from the Patent Office), a drawing of the mark, and five specimens or facsimiles. The trade-mark when approved will be your property for 20 years and may be renewed for more 20-year service periods as long as it's kept in use.

Your guide for more information is a free booklet, *General Information Concerning Trade-Marks*. For greater detail, send 40 cents to the Superintendent of Documents for *Rules of Practice in Trade-Mark Cases*.

YOUR "SECRET" NEST EGG . . .

I've saved to the end what I think is one of the most remarkable and valuable protections offered to you as a businessman by your government. It's also one of the newest; hence many businessmen either don't know much about it or haven't realized what it could mean to their future.

I'm talking about the recent provision that permits you as an employer or a self-employed person to take advantage of social-security retirement benefits. It's true! You no longer have to be employed for wages to come under the protective wing of social security. Stop at your nearest Social Security Office, or write to the Superintendent of Documents for *Social Security Information for the Self-Employed*. Your rate as a self-employed person is somewhat higher than the rate you deduct from your employee's wages, but it's still a very worth-while thing. Let's take an example at random. If you're 40 now, you only have to contribute for 10 of the 25 years you have to go to reach age 65. Since your maximum earning credit is $7,800 a year, the most you can pay into the fund is approximately $500 per year, or a total of $5,000. At 65 you begin drawing money each month for the rest of your life. If you do not survive to retirement, your widow and dependent children will draw benefits each month to help them overcome the loss of your breadwinning power. Here is one of the best forms of insurance available to the self employed.

Actually, you *don't even have to retire* to get social-security benefits but can draw reduced benefits, depending on how much you earn during a particular month. And listen to this: No matter how much you earn in a year, you will still get a *full monthly check* for any month during which your wages are under $100 or (if you're self-employed) you do not "render substantial services" to your company. And if you're over 72, even this restriction is off. You get full payment, regardless of how much work you do or what you earn!

The chances are these figures will be made more liberal as the years go by, too. So if you've had the idea that because you're the boss, you're being passed over and that social security was only for your employees, wake up!

Other booklets that will bring you up to date on this valuable protection are listed below in the Bibliography. All are free at the Social Security Office nearest you.

BIBLIOGRAPHY

Publications obtainable from the Superintendent of Documents, Washington, D.C. 20402. Free unless otherwise noted.

Copyright, Patent, Trade-Mark

Answers to Questions Frequently Asked about Patents
Copyright Office of the U.S.A.
General Information Concerning Trade-Marks
Patents and Inventions. 15 cents.
Questions and Answers about Trade-Marks
Roster of Attorneys and Agents Registered to Practice before the U.S. Patent Office. For Washington, $1.00. Local lists, free.
Rules of Practice in Trade-Mark Cases

Postal

Domestic Postage Rates and Fees
Postal Guide

Social Security

Social Security Benefits . . . How You Earn Them . . . How Much Credit You Need

Social Security Information for the Self-Employed
You Don't Have to Retire Completely to Get Social
  Security Benefits
Your Social Security

Weather

Daily Weather Map. $7.20 per year.
Monthly Weather Outlook. $4.80 per year.
Small Business Administration. *Using Weather Serv-*
  ices in Your Business. (Small Marketers Aid No.
  61.)

CHAPTER IX

UNCLE SAM AS YOUR SERVANT AND HOST

LIVING THE GOOD LIFE WITH GOVERNMENT HELP

CRADLE TO GRAVE . . .

What book has the widest sale in the United States today? Don't look at the best-seller list in your newspaper. You won't find it there.

But you can get it for 15 cents from our old friend, the Superintendent of Documents. It's called *Infant Care,* and it's the most popular government publication ever issued. Since it first came out in 1914 it has been revised more than ten times to keep up with modern developments, based on the wide experience of many doctors, pediatricians, and other experts. Many mothers across the land swear by it; they wouldn't have a baby without it!

At the other end of the rainbow of life, you can send another 15 cents for *Now that You Are Retiring.* This one discusses part-time work, activities for your suddenly expanded free time, where to live after you retire, how to make your retirement income stretch; and it also gives you some idea of the community services open to the older person.

Between these two extremes are thousands upon

thousands of government publications aimed at helping you—not only "you" the businessman whom we've been looking at so far in this book, but you, the person: the consumer, vacationer, student, hobbyist, eater, drinker, entertainer, shopper, traveler—these are all the different "yous" outside of your business life, and our government has something for all of them. In this chapter we'll throw in a grab bag of odds and ends. Just because they're not directly related to business, don't turn off your business antenna as you read about them. *Everything* is grist to the smart businessman's mill, if he keeps his eyes open. Remember the chapter on ideas; ideas are where you find them, and it could just as easily be in a pamphlet designed to tell the housewife the best way of preserving tomatoes or how to buy a new freezer.

HELP FOR THE CONSUMER . . .

While campaigning for election, the late President Kennedy announced: "The consumer is the only man in our economy without a high-powered lobbyist in Washington. I intend to be that lobbyist."

When he was elected, the President was as good as his word. In a message to Congress he said, "Consumers, by definition, include us all. They are the largest economic group in the economy, affecting and affected by almost every public and private economic decision. Two-thirds of all spending in the economy is by consumers."

He went on to describe some of the consumer's needs: to be protected from false labeling, packaging, and other sharp practices in marketing; safer transportation, food and drug protection, meat and poultry regulation, financial protection from mail frauds and exorbitant credit and interest charges, control of housing costs and quality. He stressed the need for consumer information and research as well as consumer representation in government.

This last is of special interest to us because it's what this book is about. The President said, "Too little has been done to make available to consumers the results of pertinent Government research." He ordered the creation of a Consumers' Advisory Council; also, he directed every federal agency to designate a special assistant to work on this problem; and finally, he asked the Postmaster-General to display sample government publications in the post offices and make it easier for people to buy them.

The speech is a landmark in consumer protection. You can get a copy of it from your congressman. Ask for Document No. 364 of the 87th Congress, Second Session. The program that the President outlined there had only a short time to get under way before his death. It remains to be seen whether the program is pushed ahead now or allowed to drag its feet.

UNCLE SETS A GOOD TABLE . . .

But right now, what has Uncle Sam to offer you, the consumer? Quite a bit. The Department of Agriculture alone has published more than 3,000 nontechnical booklets, most of them free, for the farmer, the housewife, the do-it-yourselfer, and just about everyone who shells out his money for food, clothing, shelter, and entertainment. Booklets tell you how to raise vegetables in the back yard, how to repair the roof, and when to spank the baby. Write to the Office of Information, U.S. Department of Agriculture, Washington 25, D.C., for a copy of *Popular Publications for the Farmer, Suburbanite, Homemaker*. Here are a few of the titles listed:

Family Fare. 35 cents.
Nutritive Value of Foods. 20 cents.
Money Saving Main Dishes. 20 cents.
Fruit and Vegetable Buying Guide. 20 cents.
Shopping Guide to U.S. Grades for Food. 10 cents.
Buying Women's Suits and Coats. 15 cents.
Men's Suits: How to Judge Quality. 35 cents.
Washing Machines, Selection and Use. 15 cents.
Detergents for Home Laundering. 5 cents.
Farmers' Handbook of Financial Calculations. 35 cents.

That last booklet gives you the dope on installment purchases, insurance, and other information you can use even if you don't happen to be a farmer. Incidentally, you can get up to ten of the pamphlets free, in spite of the listed prices.

Another Agriculture Department book you'll find extremely readable and useful—or at least your wife will —is the current hardbound *Yearbook on Food.* It is crammed with basic recipes, menus, guides, tables of nutrition values, and many money-saving suggestions. You can get it for $2.25 from the Superintendent of Documents.

While we're on agriculture, this department maintains a Special Consumer Assistant, as do most of the other departments. You can reach this official at the home office of the department, 14th Street and Independence Avenue, S.W., Washington 25, D.C. He will answer any questions you have, or he'll refer you to someone who can. Also, the Department of Agriculture runs an Institute of Home Economics. Most of the titles we've mentioned come from it. The institute is constantly experimenting and reporting on new and improved cooking methods and has a healthy interest in the housewife's budget dollar.

This department offers many services not so well known to the average citizen, and some of them are particularly interesting to the businessman. For instance, the Foreign Agricultural Service concentrates on developing foreign markets for agricultural products. It is constantly sifting marketing opportunities and aiding suppliers and others in the food industry to use them.

The Forest Service has charge of the National Forest lands, which, believe it or not, add up to about one-third of the total land area of the nation. The government is interested in seeing that our forests are not ruthlessly destroyed and goes in heavily for conservation, tree planting, and control.

The Agricultural Marketing Service does marketing research and deals in surplus food commodities. It administers the National School Lunch program which provides a midday meal and milk for millions of needy school children.

And finally, just hitting the high lights, this very important department maintains the largest government library next to the Library of Congress. You're welcome to use any of its 1,200,000 volumes on all fields of agriculture, through loans, photocopying, reference, and bibliographies. Just send the Library a query about the field you're interested in.

UNCLE TAKES YOUR TEMPERATURE . . .

If you work with epoxy resins, the government will supply a pamphlet advising you how to avoid the skin troubles such chemicals sometimes cause. That's just a sample of how Uncle Sam is concerned—and in what detail!—with keeping you alive, healthy, and contented.

Not many of us work with epoxy resins, but more common ailments are around; and the government takes notice of them. You can get a booklet on *Taking Care of Diabetes* (20 cents), for instance. When the President proclaimed April, 1963, as Cancer Control Month, the Superintendent of Documents made a special effort to acquaint the nation with the literature he had on this grim killer. Here are some of the publications featured at that time:

2H. *Cancer Cause and Prevention—Environmental Factors, Personal Factors, Occupational Hazards.* 10 cents.
3H. *Breast Self-Examination,* 10 cents.
4H. *Treating Cancer—Surgery, Radiation, Chemotherapy.* 15 cents.
5H. *Progress Against Leukemia.* 15 cents.
6H. *Cancer of the Skin.* 10 cents.
7H. *Cancer, What to Know, What to Do About It.* 5 cents.
8H. *Cancer of the Digestive Tract.* 15 cents.
9H. *Cancer of the Mouth and Respiratory Tract.* 15 cents.
10H. *Hodgkin's Disease.* 5 cents.

And for a general run-down of health and medicine, you can order the *Medical and Health Related Sciences Thesaurus* for $1.50. This book of 213 pages contains over 12,000 medical and health terms.

HE KEEPS YOU WELL . . .

The late President Kennedy's well-publicized inter-est in physical fitness resulted in a flood of printed material on the subject and saw the creation of a President's Council on Physical Fitness. Two of the best-illustrated booklets this council put out are:

1. *Physical Fitness Elements in Recreation,* which discusses fitness possibilities of individual and family participation in regular recreation programs. Lists suggested activities. 25 cents.

2. *Youth Physical Fitness,* containing recom-mendations for procedures to emphasize and improve school health programs. 40 cents.

HE SAVES YOUR LIFE . . .

One of the most valuable books you can own will cost you only one dollar. Write to the Superintendent of Documents for a copy of *Emergency Rescue Survival.* This 160-page Air Force Manual is included with the survival kit of every U.S. military airman and tells you how to get along, take care of yourself, and eventually get back in one piece under all kinds of conditions.

You don't have to be a military airman to profit by this book. Any camper, fisherman, boatman, hiker—any outdoorsman of any description—may find himself in a position where a single line from this invaluable book can mean the difference between life and death. The book is filled with illustrations, showing pictures of edible and poisonous plants, for instance, or exactly how to make an Arab-type headdress to protect you from wind or sun in the desert. The purpose of the book is to aid and insure your survival and rescue regardless of geographic location or climatic condition. The manual tells you what to do, and when, where, and how to do it, whether your survival situation be in the Arctic, desert, or tropics, on land, sea, or ice.

THE BABY DEPARTMENT . . .

The Department of Health, Education, and Welfare is the "baby department" in more ways than one. It's the newest addition to the President's Cabinet, having been created only in 1953. Its very existence is proof of the new government interest in the welfare of the consumer because, as the name implies, it is devoted to our health and our children's education and, besides, is a catchall for a number of agencies whose purpose can only be grouped under the general name of "welfare." Some agencies, such as the Public Health Service, were transferred here from other departments. This agency includes the office of the Surgeon-General and a Bureau of Medical Services (which is responsible, among other duties, for keeping the United States free of dangerous communicable diseases); it co-operates with the states in preventing, controlling, and treating disease and the elimination of hazards to health. It is not generally known that the National Library of Medicine holds the greatest collection of medical literature in the world, with over a million entries on its card index. Thousands of journals in a hundred languages are computer-coded so that a researcher can find out what has been accomplished anywhere in the world in any medical field.

READING, WRITING, AND NUCLEAR PHYSICS . . .

If you (or members of your family) are interested in vocational education, the Office of Education probably has a grant or scholarship waiting for you (or him, or her). The same thing applies to persons preparing to enter (or who have entered) the fields of "agriculture, the distributive occupations, home economics, trade and industry, practical nursing, and the fishing industry." I put quotes around that because otherwise you wouldn't believe how broad the scope is. And this is only a small sampling of the grants, scholarships, and other aids open to help young people train for occupations which the nation feels will be useful.

I've mentioned before in this book that a dollar saved is equal to the profit on ten to twenty dollars of sales. If a supplier offered you an item for a dollar less than you formerly paid, you'd grab it, wouldn't you? That is, if the quality was the same. Well, the quality of education you get on government grant is identical with the kind you shell out $250 to $2,500 per year for—at the same schools and colleges, and under the same teachers.

So, if any member of your family is going to school or plans to go, send to the Office of Education, Department of Health, Education, and Welfare, 330 Independence Avenue, S.W., Washington, D.C., for a list of the grants and scholarships, with requirements and applications, that may be offered in any particular field of study.

For instance, under the Fulbright Act thousands of Americans study abroad each year or do teaching or research in foreign countries. There are other special fellowships for Latin America, Finland; and there's financial aid for undergraduate students and summer students abroad.

The National Science Foundation, Atomic Energy Commission, and Public Health Service also offer help to students, trainees, and research scholars. And don't forget the giant work of the G.I. Education and Training Program. About ten million veterans have taken advantage of G.I. schooling to complete their education and to get special training in many fields.

YOUR BOOKSTORE! . . .

The Library of Congress will see that any serious student gets any book or other materials in its vast collection. The Library has over 30 million items on file, including maps, photographs, phonograph records, sheet music—anything that can be printed. Through modern microfilm and photoduplication methods, you can get the benefit of whatever you need without taking the trip to Washington.

SOCIAL SECURITY . . .

The really important agency of HEW (Health, Education, and Welfare), as far as you—a businessman and consumer—are concerned, is the gigantic and growing Social Security Administration. If you draw a pay check, you are familiar with the famous "deducts," one of which is for your Old-Age and Survivor's Insurance. We talked about this in Chapter VIII as it applied to the self-employed person. If you're employed, the provisions are the same, except that the payment is shared by your employerand doesn't cost you as much.

Whether you work for yourself or for a boss, it will

pay you to study your rights and benefits under this program. Go to your nearest Social Security Office and pick up Leaflet No. 855, *Social Security Benefits.* This tells you how you earn them, how much credit you need to get the benefits, how to estimate the amount of benefit you'll be getting when you retire, and at what age.

The "survivor" part of social security means that the widow or widower of a social-security beneficiary also gets support in the form of a lump sum at the death of the breadwinner and monthly payments for widow and minor children.

IF YOU BECOME DISABLED . . .

This is the title of another social-security booklet you should look into. You can get a copy at the nearest Social Security Office. It tells you how long you must have worked under social security to get benefits, how seriously disabled you must be, and how to make your application.

Some other social-security pamphlets you can get free are:

Financing Your Social Security Benefits
Your Social Security Earnings Record
Social Security for Servicemen and Veterans
Social Security Information for Self-Employed Farmers
How Social Security Works for Non-Profit Organizations and Their Employees
Good News for Household Workers
Social Security and Your Household Employee
If You Work While You Get Social Security Payments
Now that You Are Retiring

KIDDIE DEPARTMENT . . .

The Children's Bureau was transferred to Health, Education, and Welfare when this new department was created. It doesn't provide direct care of children, but many a mother has raised a child on the pamphlet *Infant Care* we spoke about earlier. About eight and a half million copies of this little manual have been distributed, and I'd guess that one child in three in this nation has benefited from it. The Children's Bureau publishes other valuable pamphlets and books, some popular, some technical. Here are a few of the most useful titles:

Prenatal Care
Your Child From One to Six
Your Child From Six to Twelve
The Adolescent in Your Family
Your Gifted Child
A Healthy Personality For Your Child
The Mentally Retarded Child at Home
Nutrition and Healthy Growth
Children of Working Mothers
Handbook for Recreation
Your Children and Their Gangs

There are seventeen additional pamphlets on *Facts and Facets of Delinquency*, and the bureau puts out a bimonthly magazine, *Children*. You can get copies of all these for the asking. Apply to the Children's Bureau at the local or Washington address of HEW.

And these are not dry-as-dust government-type pamphlets, either. In the joyous spirit which seems to infect all who work with and around children, even the staid old Government Printing Office gets into the act! An example is a series called *Headliners*. One of these is a *Pogo Primer for Parents* (*TV Division*), in which Walt Kelly's delightful cartoon characters advise parents on how to handle the problem of television watching in relation to children. It warns parents against letting the TV set "watch the children," takes up the matter of violence and frightening elements, and concludes: "Do not wind your child up and set him to watch the TV set unguided. Do not wind the TV set up and set it to watch the child. A machine is bad as a sole companion. It needs help. You can help it. Love your child."

HOME, SWEET HOME . . .

There was a time when you had to save up in advance and produce 50 per cent or more as a down payment to buy a house. Or you floated the first 50 per cent with a ruinous second—and sometimes third—mortgage. Mortgages were written with a gigantic "balloon" payment at the end which hung over your head until the last cent was paid. Your home could be snatched away from you. Naturally, under these conditions, homeownership was a "sometime thing," and then only for the upper crust of the financial pie.

Later, largely due to federal education of bankers and others, it was realized that a man would lose his shirt before he'd risk losing his home—that the homeowner was the safest risk on record. Bankers loosened up. Then came the Federal Housing Authority, willing to lend up to 97 per cent on a housing loan. No more second and third mortgages, no more balloon payments. Result: You and I and the man who hauls the garbage can own a home, too! Actually, the FHA does not lend the money; it merely insures the bank or lending organization against the loans they make to homeowners. In so doing, however, the FHA calls the shots, keeping interest low and down-payment figures to a reasonable amount, and—what is probably just as important—insists on high standards in housing construction and conditions.

Here are some of the books you can pick up at lending institutions or FHA offices or can write for to the Office of Public Information, Federal Housing Administration, Washington 25, D.C. They're all free.

FHA Mortgage Insurance
Estimating Your Ability to Pay For a Home
FHA Home Owner's Guide
FHA and the Home-Buying Serviceman

For a complete run-down on what Uncle Sam can offer you to make your home cheaper, safer, healthier, and happier, write to the Superintendent of Documents for PL 72, *Homes*.

BE MY GUEST! . . .

Uncle Sam maintains hundreds of vacation spots for you to enjoy. As an American citizen, you're part owner of the hundreds of millions of acres of mountain, forest, desert, and seashore lands comprising the National Park and National Forest systems. Two hundred national parks await your pleasure, each one offering its own individual attractions, from the bears and geysers of Yellowstone to the mysterious swampland of the Everglades. You have the Grand Canyon, Bryce Canyon, Mt. Rainier and its glaciers, Crater Lake, the Grand Tetons in the West and Abraham Lincoln's birthplace, the Cumberland Gap, the Edison Laboratory in West Orange, New Jersey, and hundreds of other historical and scenic spots in the East. They cover our country; there's bound to be one or more near you. The list is a fascinating treasurehouse of infinite variety. You have Uncle's word that these jewels will never be overrun with high-rise apartments, disfigured by billboards, or priced out of the reach of your pocket-book. The government controls food and lodging prices and provides informed and courteous rangers to help you have fun, whether your idea of fun is fishing, hiking, swimming, driving, camping, or just plain loafing. No hunting and no guns are allowed within national-park borders; and this is the reason the numerous animals and birds are so tameand unafraid.

As an old national-park vacationer, I can't urge you strongly enough to try out Uncle's hospitality if you've never done so. Send to the National Park Service, Department of the Interior, for two booklets describing all the parks and monuments in the system. One covers the eastern United States, the other the West. You'll be briefed on the extent of the open season, the facilities, exhibits, accommodations (which range from camping and tourist cabins to luxury hotels like the Ahwanee in Yosemite), the activities, guided trips, and other information you'll want.

During your stay, you'll be treated like a king—or should I say landlord? You'll get a breath of fresh air, and nature in its most beautiful state will spread before you; you'll come home refreshed and renewed.

Do I sound a little wild? I've been accused of conducting a love affair with the Government Printing Office; let's say the National Park Service is my second light o' love, and that won't be far wrong!

THE WELCOME MAT'S OUT FOR YOU . . .

For an entirely different kind of vacation, still with Uncle as host, try visiting him at home. Plan a visit to Washington, D.C. There are few more exciting spots in the nation than its capital, the center and focus of all the department activity we've been talking about. Before you go, send for two pamphlets to get acquainted with what you'll see in this city of magnificence, beauty, and history. *Know Your Capital City* (25 cents) and *Our Capitol* (30 cents) are fascinating to read, even if you never get to go to Washington. The first tells all about Washington's colorful history and gives you the descriptions and information on the famous landmarks and government buildings. The second book details the story of the Capitol Building. You learn how and when it was originally built and how it grew to its present form. All the history and tradition of its paintings, murals, statues, and furnishings is told. Both books are illustrated.

You'll also want the *U.S. Government Organization Manual* ($1.50) to make your Washington visit more complete. This official organizational handbook of 761 pages and illustrations tells all about every department, bureau, and agency of our government: where it is, who operates it, what it does. It's a valuable reference book you'll find useful in many ways.

Here, too, you are reminded at every turn that *you* own the place. Most of the public buildings are open for touring, from the White House and the Capitol to the big GPO itself.

HOBBY LOBBY . . .

Perhaps you feel that this chapter has wandered away from the original theme of our book, which is "business." Not at all; for keep in mind that you're more than just a businessman; you're a whole man (or woman), and outside interests are just as important to keeping you going in business as, well, eating. Sir William Osler, the famous physician, said, "No man is really happy or safe without a hobby, and it makes precious little difference what the outside interest may be—botany, beetles or butterflies; roses, tulips or irises; fishing, mountaineering, or antiques—anything will do so long as he straddles a hobby and rides it hard."

Hobbies can *directly* influence and help your business, too. A talent for golf has put many a man farther ahead than his business ability warranted.

Collect stamps? Given a big boost by F.D.R., who was a stamp collector of the first water, the Philatelic Agency of the Post Office Department takes in a nice clear profit of up to 5 or 6 million dollars a year from stamps that will never travel on an envelope. These, of course, are picked up by people who make stamp collecting their hobby. The government knows that collectors will flock to the post office for blocks and sheets of every new commemorative issue that comes out, and so plenty are issued. The nice thing about collecting uncanceled United States stamps is supposed to be that you can almost always get your money out if you change your mind about keeping them. Don't count on this. Certainly you won't get it from the post office. They won't take back stamps, for sanitary reasons. You'll have to find a company to buy them from you for commercial use, and you'll have to offer a hefty discount. With more and more big companies using precanceled mail, that market is shrinking. The only alternative is to send out a heck of a lot of Christmas cards yourself!

Profit from stamps? Sure, if you know your stamps. There's a superstition going round that if you had bought a sheet of every issue put out from the time you were old enough to reach the post-office counter, you'd have a fortune in stamps today because of the rarity value. This, unfortunately, is not true. Some issues have advanced on the collecting market; but stamps are put out in such mountainous quantity that very few of them have a chance to become rare within your lifetime.

However, don't let that stop you from collecting or teaching the youngster to collect. There's no more fascinating and educational hobby open to the person of modest income. Read up on the subject, learn the angles, and you'll have your fun and profit, too.

Coins are a different matter. They're always good for face value and inevitably go up at least a little with the years because, as time goes by, fewer and fewer remain in proof, mint, or fine condition. The mint sells proof sets each year; a set consisting of a cent, nickel, dime, quarter, and half-dollar may be ordered from the Superintendent of the Mint, Philadelphia 30, Pennsylvania. Each set costs $2.10, because of the special handling necessary. Any coin dealer will show you how to preserve the beautiful satin finish of the coins by mounting them in plastic. And you can watch them grow slowly but surely in value over the years.

Like stamps, coins are more fun if you know all about them. Read up on the subject. A good beginning is two free publications you can get from the Bureau of the Mint, Washington 25, D.C., called *Facts about United States Money* and *Coins and Currency of The United States*.

AND OTHERS . . .

Stamp and coin collecting are just two popular hobbies that come to mind immediately. But without looking the matter up, I'm willing to venture that you couldn't take up a hobby in which the government doesn't offer you some help. To step up the status scale, I have a handsome book put out by the Smithsonian Institution, *Automobiles and Motorcycles*. It contains 150-odd slick-paper pages of description and illustrations, many in color, of the museum's collection of classic automobiles and cycles, dating back to 1869! This collection includes the Duryea car, thought to be the first American automobile driven by an internal-combustion engine. Names like Haynes, Apperson, Daimler, stud the magnificent collection described here. If a serious car collector were asked to choose one car he could take out and own, he'd without doubt go for the Simplex Speed chain-drive. It represents all that is grand in the cars of the brassbound era, a truly mighty engine and beautiful clean lines. Only a few of these cars remain intact today, and the Smithsonian has the best of them.

This booklet is National Museum Bulletin No. 213 and may be had free from the National Museum, Washington, D.C.

WANT TO SPEAK IBO? . . .

A course in Ibo, first of the basic African languages published, has just been placed on sale by the Superintendent of Documents. Ibo is the principal language of the Eastern Region of Nigeria and is spoken by some four million people. The course represents a pioneer effort to apply the results of linguistic analysis and teaching experience to the special problems of a complex tonal language of West Africa and at least partially fills an urgent need for instructional materials in this language. You can get the complete basic course for $2.25.

Or how about French, German, or Spanish? Many basic language courses are offered by the Superintendent of Documents. They range anywhere from $2.00 to $7.50

per set, and even tape recordings can be purchased to supplement these excellent textbooks. In addition, you can purchase *A Guide for the Teaching of French in the Elementary Schools* and a similar one for Spanish. These two publications were prepared for the use of teachers in the public elementary schools of the District of Columbia for teaching French and Spanish to children in the kindergarten through the sixth grade. Each book provides a vocabulary chart directly related to a child's everyday experiences at play, in the community, and in the school, aids to pronunciation and usage, a list of personal names, suggested procedures, and songs and verses in the language for each grade level.

TO SUM UP . . .

Since hobbies are as numerous as people, I won't try to go into more detail here. All I need say is, if you've kept reading up to this point, you should be pretty well convinced, as I am, that whatever your interest, from archery to zoology, from coin collecting to foreign languages, you can get help, information, instruction, and encouragement from our government's vast storehouse.

BIBLIOGRAPHY

Source: Superintendent of Documents, Washington, D.C. 20402

Infant Care. 15 cents
Now that You Are Retiring. 15 cents.
Yearbook on Food. $2.25.
Medical and Health Related Sciences Thesaurus. $1.50.
Physical Fitness Elements in Recreation. 25 cents.
Youth Physical Fitness. 40 cents.
Prenatal Care

Your Child From One to Six
Your Child From Six to Twelve
The Adolescent in Your Family
Your Gifted Child
A Healthy Personality For Your Child
The Mentally Retarded Child at Home
Nutrition and Healthy Growth
Children of Working Mothers
Handbook for Recreation
Your Children and Their Gangs
Facts and Facets of Delinquency
Children (bimonthly magazine)
Pogo Primer for Parents (TV Division)

Source: U.S. Department of Agriculture, Washington 25, D.C.

Family Fare. 35 cents.
Nutritive Value of Foods. 20 cents.
Money Saving Main Dishes. 20 cents.
Fruit and Vegetable Buying Guide. 20 cents.
Shopping Guide to U.S. Grades for Food. 10 cents.
Buying Women's Suits and Coats. 15 cents.
Men's Suits: How to Judge Quality. 35 cents.
Washing Machines, Selection and Use. 15 cents.
Detergents for Home Laundering. 5 cents.
Financing Your Social Security Benefits
Your Social Security Earnings Record
Farmers' Handbook of Financial Calculations. 35 cents.

Source: Federal Housing Administration, Washington 25, D.C.

FHA Mortgage Insurance
Estimating Your Ability to Pay For a Home
FHA Home Owner's Guide
FHA and the Home-Buying Serviceman

Superintendent of Documents. PL 72, *Homes.*

Social Security for Servicemen and Veterans
Social Security Information for Self-Employed Farmers
How Social Security Works for Non-Profit Organizations. Cf. 25 cents.
Good News for Household Workers
Social Security and Your Household Employee
If You Work While You Get Social Security Payments

Know Your Capital City. 25 cents.
Our Capitol. 30 cents.
U.S. Government Organization Manual. $1.50.

The National Park System: Eastern United States
The National Park System: Western United States
Wilderness—America's Playgrounds. 20 cents.

U.S. Department of Agriculture, Forest Service. National-Forest Vacations.
Emergency Rescue—Survival. $1.00.

Ibo—Basic Course. $2.25.
N. 14. *A Guide for the Teaching of French in the Elementary Schools.* 75 cents.
No. 15. *A Guide for the Teaching of Spanish in the Elementary Schools.* 75 cents.
No. 16. *A Practical Spanish Grammar for Border Patrol Officers.* $1.00.
No. 17. *Dictionary of Spoken Spanish.* $1.75.

Automobiles and Motorcycles in the U.S. National Museum. (U.S. National Museum Bulletin No. 213.) Free.

CHAPTER X

UNCLE SAM'S BARGAIN STORE

A Treasure of Information
with Government Publications

OPEN SESAME!

When Aladdin first set foot inside the treasure cave, he didn't stop to make a catalogue of the goodies it contained. He didn't classify the pearls for size and luster, the gold for fineness, the diamonds for carat weight. He didn't have to, because he realized he'd stepped into something the like of which the world had never seen, and it all was his for the taking.

Well, this is somewhat the feeling I got when I first heard about the Government Printing Office, and it's a feeling I hope you've shared by reading this book. Actually, you have to visit the GPO to realize its gigantic scope and sheer size. It's an eight-story building with over 32 acres of floor space where giant high-speed presses turn out over 140,000,000 books and pamphlets each year. Some 54,000,000 of these are sold for a nickel up; and 86,000,000 more are distributed *free*. Order clerks fill orders or answer inquiries amounting to 1,500,000 a year: 9,000 a day! Besides the mail business, there's a real bookstore where you can browse around yourself, examining the literature available.

And incidentally, as a businessman, you'll be happy to learn that the GPO runs at a profit. While trying to price the books as near cost as possible, the office, every year, turns back to the United States Treasury a surplus of around $5,000,000 left over after expenses and rebuilding stocks are satisfied.

THE LAST ROUNDUP . . .

You can see from the size of the GPO store that, like Aladdin, I couldn't begin to classify and bring to you in this book one hundreth part of their offerings. In the preceding chapters I've only tried to whet your appetite so you could find out more for yourself. Weekly, the mailman brings me lists of new items put out by the various departments and agencies. If I waited for the last of them, this book would never see print; so a halt has to be called somewhere. However, I can't drop the matter without giving you a final glimpse of the fantastic variety of the publications that pour out of the GPO. So, without apology, here's one last free-for-all, hodge-podge bag of books. Not all of them will be of interest to you, of course. But you'll surely find something in the bunch to make you sit up and read! So, grab your hat . . . hold on . . . and let's go!

Let's start with "the top twenty-five"—the twenty-five best sellers at the GPO, which by their continuous response have shown that they fill real needs of the people. We've already told you about a few of them, but there's nothing here that won't bear a little repetition.

1. *Food, The Yearbook of Agriculture.* This yearbook on food contains simple basic recipes, menus, food guides, tables of nutritive value and calories.

What to eat for better health and greater energy, how to gain or lose weight, how to stretch your food dollar, how to plan and cook meals your family needs and enjoys, which foods babies, children, teen-agers and adults need, and much more. $2.25.

2. *Family Fare*. Packed with facts about foods and cooking—nutrition guides, food plans, buying and storage hints, menu aids, and many tasty recipes—this useful pamphlet has been prepared specially for the homemaker. It includes a complete index of these recipes, a list of cooking terms, suggestions on ways to use leftovers, and a list of ingredients that can be substituted for those not immediately on hand. 35 cents.

3. *Nutritive Value of Foods*. Presents three tables on the food values in about 500 foods commonly used in this country, the yield of cooked meat per pound of raw meat, and recommended daily dietary allow-ances. 20 cents.

4. *Food and Your Weight*. The calorie values in common foods, a table of the desirable weights for men and women, and brief discussion of the body's daily calorie need and some basic weight-control facts. In addition, it includes suggestions for reducers and for those who want to gain weight and helpful ideas for planning a day's food. 15 cents.

5. *Wood Handbook*. Designed as an aid to better and more efficient use of wood, this volume covers the structure of wood, physical properties of wood, grades and sizes of lumber, gluing of wood, plywood and other cross-banded products, control of moisture and shrinkage of wood, painting and finishing of wood, fire resistance of wood construction, wood preservation, heat insulation, and many other informa-tive facts about wood. $2.25.

6. *Removing Stains from Fabrics, Home Methods*. Provides up-to-date information on removing stains

from various types of fabrics, including stain-removal suggestions for the newer man-made fibers and those with special finishes. It describes the proper use of the four types of stain removers—absorbent material, detergents, solvents, and bleaches—and other chemical stain removers. Specific directions for removing all kinds of individual stains. 15 cents.

7. _Starting and Managing a Small Business of Your Own._ Describes the common problems of launching small business operations in general, suggesting specific steps to help those interested in starting and managing a small business to arrive at sound decisions concerning these problems. 25 cents.

8. _Our Growing Population._ This graphic 12-page pamphlet presents in popular form data taken primarily from the detailed reports on Number of Inhabitants, Series PC(1)-A, of the 1960 Census of Population. It explains the growth of America's population, providing information on births and deaths, immigration, population and land expansion, and state population increases. It also compares our people against others in the world and gives an estimate of what our population may be by 1970 and 1980. 10 cents.

9. _Manual on Uniform Traffic Control Devices for Streets and Highways._ Widely accepted and time-tested traffic-control practices in the design and application of control devices, as well as extensive research into the principles of safe and orderly movement of vehicles and pedestrians. It includes specific standards for expressway signing, a major section on signing and marking for contracting and maintenance operations, and a brief treatment of civil-defense signing. $2.00.

10. _U.S. Income and Output._ Income and product data give a comprehensive account of our postwar economic expansion. The text includes an analysis

of the American economy as viewed through the national income accounts over the past quarter-century and of the needed directions of future research. $1.50.

11. *Our Flag*. Unfolding many historical facts about our flag, this booklet relates the story of the Stars and Stripes; brief notes on various early American flags; instructions on displaying the flag; and approved flag customs. 25 cents.

12. *Your Social Security*. Describing your social-security rights and responsibilities, this booklet provides details on retirement, survivors, and disability payments; amount of work required; events that stop payments; kinds of work covered; procedure for checking your account; and other helpful information. 10 cents.

13. *Infant Care*. The most popular government publication ever issued, this book revised ten times since it first appeared in 1914, provides the information needed by parents in caring for their baby, especially a first baby. Based on the experience of many doctors, pediatricians, nurses, child-development and other experts, it is designed to help parents understand many phases of infant care, such as feeding, clothing, care, growth and development of the baby. 15 cents.

14. *Your Baby's First Year*. This short picture leaflet on the care of a baby for his first year of life is designed for quick reading and covers the most important points in good baby care. In its 32 pages it discusses briefly the baby's needs, such as foods, vitamins, sleep, love, play, and clothes; his growth and development; signs of sickness; and other points of similar interest. 15 cents.

15. *First Aid*. Beginning with an explanation of the principles of first aid and a discussion of the human anatomy this pocket-sized Bureau of Mines

manual gives detailed, well-illustrated instructions on dealing with serious bleeding; stoppage of breath, poisoning, shock, fractures and dislocations, sprains, strains, wounds and bandaging, fainting snake bites, burns and scalds, and many, many other injuries and emergencies. 60 cents.

16. *How to Get and Hold the Right Job.* Gives some of the basic elements of getting and holding a job. 10 cents.

17. *Choosing Your Occupation.* Provides guides and a self-inventory to help high-school students determine what occupation is right for them. 15 cents.

18. *Job Guide for Young Workers.* Presents detailed descriptions of duties and characteristics, qualifications required, employment prospects, advancement opportunities, and sources of employment for more than one hundred jobs frequently held by young people entering the labor force from high school. Also contains general employment-outlook information, tips on how to go about getting a job, and other useful facts. 45 cents.

19. *Future Jobs for High School Girls.* Designed for high-school graduates, their counselors, and their parents, this pamphlet describes the job future of these young women and provides information on a variety of occupations open to women, from the woman-dominated secretarial group to technical specialties where women are just beginning to make their mark. 40 cents.

20. *Astronaut John H. Glenn Orbits the Earth for America, February 20, 1962.* Pictorially this publication presents a short résumé of the events of this historical day from the time he arose at 2:20 A.M. until the touchdown in the ocean southeast of Cape Canaveral at 2:43 P.M. and the recovery of the astronaut and the capsule. It also includes a condensation from the transcript of Colonel Glenn's remarks at his

press conference at Cape Canaveral, February 23, 1962, and photographs of some of the events honoring Colonel Glenn after his orbital flight. 15 cents.

21. *Effective Revenue Writing 1.* A basic course designed to give a brief, practical review of writing principles, grammar, and punctuation, this volume presents grammar in a practical way by showing the functions of words or how they may be used. It covers sentence sense, naming words, agreement and reference, tense of verbs and verbals, mood and voice, modifiers, connectives, punctuation and good sentences, word relationships, the effective sentence, and a writer's guide to current usage of some words and phrases. $1.00.

22. *Effective Revenue Writing 2.* An advanced course designed to help experienced writers and reviewers diagnose and cure writing weaknesses. It discusses the nature and function of written communication, the significant diagnosing of sentence deficiencies, the role of grammar in writing, the semantic problem, putting words to work, the syntax of strong sentences, economy in writing, using modifiers effectively, parallelism, linkage, logic and syntax, and style in expository writing. 70 cents.

23. *Federal Benefits for Veterans and Dependents.* This fact sheet is designed to provide *only* general information concerning most federal benefits enacted by the Congress of the United States for veterans, their dependents, and their beneficiaries. It discusses benefits for veterans of the Spanish-American War, World Wars I and II, Korean conflict, peacetime veterans, six-month enlistees, and for those in active service. 20 cents.

24. *Guide to Subversive Organizations and Publications (and Appendixes).* This guide is basically a compilation of organizations and publications which have been declared to be Communist-front or out-

right Communist enterprises in official statements by federal legislative and executive authorities and by various state and territorial investigating committees. 70 cents.

25. *Outdoor Recreation for America.* Surveys our country's outdoor recreation resources, measures present and likely demands upon them over the next forty years, and recommends actions to insure their availability to all Americans of present and future generations. Chapters on special problems of management, financing, water, and research are included. Extensive use of graphics and photographs, and a comprehensive, cross-referenced index add to the completeness and interest of the text, $2.50.

USE REVERSE ENGLISH . . .

Before going on, I want to caution you once more, as I have done throughout this book, to look at the references with a broad and, if I may use the word, creative eye. There's every likelihood you'll get out of them something that even the writer or the bureau which put them out never thought of.

Let me give you an example. The Department of agriculture has a publication called the *Cooperative Economic Insect Report.* This comes from the Plant Pest Control Division and is basically designed to help farmers, industrial entomologists, and "other agricultural workers," as the Foreword clearly states. I don't suppose the creators of this important but highly specialized bit of literature had any other views of its usefulness when they described a decrease in citrus mites in Florida and an increase in green-peach aphids in Arizona. Certainly, they never expected it to be avidly read by a city boy who wouldn't know which end of a hoe was which.

Nevertheless, I read it regularly. Why? Because, as I've mentioned before, one of our best-selling mail-order items is a fly killer called Fly Cake. From this periodical, describing the activities of insects in various parts of the country, we learn where the housefly is on the upgrade, and we concentrate our advertising in those areas to get maximum effect. So you see, it *is* possible to make a silk purse out of a sow's earwig; all you need is a little imagination!

WATCH THE BIRDIE . . .

A photography magazine had some mighty nice words to say about the series of books the Air Force and the Navy have put out to train photographers. They're not primers, but textbooks. Each chapter has quizzes and problems to help you keep up with the material. To an eager camera bug who wants to learn more about his hobby, these books are pure gold. Here they are:

Basic Photography, Air Force Manual 95-1, No.D 301.7:95-1. $2.00.

Handbook for Photo Lab Processing. No.D.301.7: 95-11. $4.75. No. D.301.7:95-11A (updating supplement to above). 20 cents.

Installation and Maintenance of Aerial Photographic Equipment, Air Force Manual 95-3, No.D.301.7: 95-3. $3.00.

Method for Determining Resolving Power of Photographic Lenses. No.C 13, 4:533. $1.75.

Military Standardization Handbook, Glossary of Photographic Terms, D7.6/2.25. 70 cents.

Photographer's Mate 2, No. D 208.11:P 56/4. $2.25.

Photographer's Mate 3, No. D 208.11:P 56/3/961.
$3.00.

Photographer's Mate 1 & C, No. D 208.11.P 56/5.
$2.25.

Electric Current Abroad, U.S. Dept. of Commerce
Publication. 25 cents.

A FEW MORE HOBBYHORSES . . .

Raising Rabbits. Nice pets; good stew, too! 20
cents.

Hamster Raising. Not for eating, but they can be
both fun and a business. 5 cents.

Weather Forecasting. You, too, can be cussed
out by your friends when you make a mistake! 25
cents.

Ducks at a distance. A must for sportsmen, students, bird watchers, this book colorfully portrays
the waterfowl in the attitudes you'll most commonly
see them take. It tells you what to look for in identi-
fying shapes, colors, voices, flight patterns, rising
views, and flock formations. 25 cents.

Backpacking in the National Forest Wilderness.
Written for those city folk who dream of exploring
the vast wilds but don't quite know how. It tells
how to choose equipment, gives sample menus, lists
organizations where you can get more information.
And it lists by states the wilderness-type areas of the
national forests for you to choose from. 15 cents.

Attracting Birds. Tells you how to bring the
beautiful feathered folk to your home, how to feed,
water, and protect them, and how to see that you
don't overdo it, since there are hazards (for man and
the birds) in too great a concentration. 15 cents.

Migration of Birds. Another book for the bird-
man: the how, where, and when of bird travel, routes

they take, and lots more, all written by experts, as are all these books. 35 cents.

Recreational Boating Guide. Takes up the growing sport of boating. You get federal laws, guidelines for safe and enjoyable cruising, even what to do in an emergency. 40 cents. And while we're on the water:

Harbor Craft Crewman's Handbook. Designed for crew members of the U.S. Transportation Corps, but just as valuable to the private boatman or boat-owner. You'll read about small-boat and ship handling, piloting, tows and towing, construction, watches and drills, weather, rules of the road, machinery, cargo—no end of information. $1.50. Also:

The National Watercraft Collection. Written by a leading marine historian, illustrated, it tells about the big watercraft collection of the Smithsonian Institution. Merchant sail, merchant steam, and fishing ·craft are described; photographs: plans of old ships, drawn from the collection of builder's models. This is a real collector's item in itself. $3.50.

SHOCKING NEWS . . .

Starting at my own level of knowledge about electricity, electronics, radar, and radio—which is rock bottom—you can learn *How to Keep Electricity from Killing You* (35 cents) in a humorously illustrated booklet put out originally for Navy personnel. From there on you can go into the stratosphere and beyond, with titles like:

Electrical Fundamentals (Alternating Current). $1.25.
Electrical Fundamentals (Direct Current). $1.00.
FM Transmitters and Receivers. $1.50.
Troubleshooting and Repair of Radio Equipment. $2.00.

Radio Frequency Control in Space Telecommunications. 75 cents.

International Morse Code (Instructions). 25 cents.

Climatic Charts and Data, Etc. (Cloth) $2.00.

Standard Frequencies and Time Signals, Etc. 10 cents.

Communication Satellites, Etc. $1.00.

Introduction to Electronics. 35 cents.

Basic Electronics. $2.85.

Handbook of Miniature Parts for Electronic Equipment. $2.00.

English-Russian, Russian-English Electronics Dictionary. $3.50.

NO LONGER FOR LOVERS . . .

The nations of the world are casting a cold eye on the moon with an idea of dividing it up into real estate. Our own country, never backward in enterprise, is ready to sell you—believe it or not—*Charts of the Moon!* That's right, dear reader! The Air Force has charted the moon in extremely fine detail at a scale of one inch to 16 miles and sells it off in sections (charts, that is) 22 by 29 inches each, and in color. You can order your charts at $5.50 per subscription, pick out your vacation spot, and head for it by the next rocket!

Meanwhile, before you blast off, you can watch out underfoot for *Poisonous Snakes of the World* ($2.00), put out to save Navy personnel, wherever they might be, from the most dangerous species of serpents. It has numerous colored photographs of the most typical and common species.

Going down nature's path, you can get books on:

Grass. Devoted to grassland agriculture, this yearbook discusses the needs and uses of the more common grasses and legumes as well as the place of grasses, legumes, and associated plants in animal feeding, conservation, crop rotation, farm management, soil building, and other related fields. (Cloth) $2.00.

Trees. Tells how and why to plant trees and care for them; explains the essentials of choosing, planting, and growing trees as a farm crop, as a renewable natural treasure, and as a necessary part of city and country life. It has chapters on specific problems or values: insects, fire, recreation, wildlife, forestry, and economic importance. (Cloth) $2.75.

Water. Presents a series of articles by outstanding authorities on a subject that is of interest to everyone. Among the many topics covered are: water and soil conservation; irrigation; industry's need for water; water pollution; weather cycles; floods; water and wildlife; safe water supplies; and water laws. (Cloth) $2.25.

Soil. In 800 fact-filled pages, 142 leading authorities tell you what you want to know about such subjects as soil structures and types; fertilizers; organic matter; compost, mulches; economies of moisture; soil management in your region; soil management for gardens, lawns, flowers, vegetables; and many more. (Cloth) $2.25.

Land. Gives a wealth of information about our vast public domain; the increasing sizes of farms and our declining farm population; government programs; Indian lands; land in Alaska and Hawaii, our two new states, and Puerto Rico; land in subdivisions; highways; tenure; irrigation; forests; and a host of other related subjects. (Cloth) $2.25.

Seeds. In well-written informative chapters, this unique book presents the complete story of seeds: why seeds are important to you; how seeds develop, travel, rest, grow, and carry life onward; how men produce, improve, clean, store, test, certify, and sell seeds of all kinds; what modern science has learned about the effect on seed production of various factors; what all buyers of seeds should know about seed laws, frauds, good and poor seeds, weeds, costs. (Cloth) $2.00.

And to wrap all this up, there's:

After a Hundred Years. What does the agricultural revolution of this century mean? How does it affect me? This Centennial Yearbook answers these questions in 108 chapters and hundreds of pictures. It is a treasure of information about outstanding developments in farm practices, scientific methods, plants, conservation, forests, animals, insects, machines, food, clothing, markets, trade, books, homes, and problems we all face. It is a book about people. It is for everyone who wants a better understanding of our changing world, for everyone who loves the country. (Cloth) $3.00.

PLANNING YOUR FUTURE WITH GOVERNMENT HELP

Choosing a career? Changing jobs? Counseling others about these decisions? The facts are at your fingertips in a 792-page reference book on nearly seven hundred occupations and thirty major industries. This reference book is called *Occupational Outlook Handbook* and sells for $4.75 from the Superintendent of Documents, Government Printing Office, Washington, D.C. 20402.

If you are only interested in a particular field, you can buy any one of dozens of reports from accountants, advertising, or architects to railroads, restaurants, or television and radio broadcasting. These occupational outlook reports range in price from five cents each to fifteen cents each and can really help you to decide on what career to follow. These reports are invaluable to parents, students, teachers, employees; etc.

A LOOK AT HISTORY . . .

The United States has a long and glorious history, and Uncle Sam wants all his nephews and nieces to know as much about it as possible. So that you can own the basic documents of our nation, he offers you a set of facsimile reproductions of the Nation's Charters of Freedom. The Constitution, the Bill of Rights, and the Declaration of Independence are now available on three pages suitable for framing. These three facsimiles, prepared from the parchments on display in the National Archives at Washington, D.C., faithfully reproduce the yellowish tint and faded brown ink of the originals. The four sheets of the Constitution have been reduced and reproduced on one large page. The Bill of Rights and the Declaration of Independence are about the same size as the original documents. Copies of these freedom documents should also be a worth-while addition to every American home. The individual documents are priced:

The Bill of Rights (facsimile). 33 by 31 inches. 45 cents.
The Constitution of the United States (facsimile). 38 by 31 inches. 45 cents.
The Declaration of Independence (facsimile). 35 by 29 inches. 45 cents.
Or you can order a set of all three Charters of Freedom for $1.35.

Going ahead in our history, you can follow the pioneers step by step through thirty-six fascinating booklets covering events and describing historical places. The titles in this Historical Handbook Series are:

Custer Battlefield (Montana). The story of General Custer and the battlefield where he made his "last stand." 20 cents.

Jamestown (Virginia). The first permanent English settlement in America. 25 cents.

The Lincoln Museum and the House Where Lincoln Died (District of Columbia). Portrays the story and scene of the assassination of Abraham Lincoln. 25 cents.

Saratoga (New York). The defeat of the British forces at Saratoga may be considered to mark the turning point of the American Revolution. 25 cents.

Fort McHenry (Maryland). Gives the events of history surrounding the birth of our National Anthem. 25 cents.

Custis-Lee Mansion, The Robert E. Lee Memorial (Virginia). The history of the home of Robert E. Lee. 25 cents.

Morristown (New Jersey). The story of two critical winters of the Revolutionary War. 30 cents.

Hopewell Village (Pennsylvania). Tells about the establishment of the early American iron industry. 25 cents.

Gettysburg (Pennsylvania). Relates the history, campaign, and Battle of Gettysburg. The story of the establishment and dedication of the cemetery and the events leading to the famous "Gettysburg Address" delivered by Lincoln. 25 cents.

Shiloh (Tennessee). Scene of the first major engagement in the western campaign of the War Between the States, this handbook describes the preliminary campaign and the first two days' battles on April 6 and 7, 1862, and gives the results of the battle at Shiloh. 25 cents.

Statue of Liberty (New York). Gives the story of one of the most symbolic structures in the United States. 25 cents.

Fort Sumter (South Carolina). Describes in detail the construction of Fort Sumter, the events leading to the firing of the "first shot" of the Civil War, and the Federal bombardments of the fort from 1863 to 1865. 25 cents.

Petersburg (Virginia). Tells of the fighting which centered around Petersburg, the scene of decisive military operations that cut the Confederate lines of communications between Richmond and the South and led to the capture of the Confederate capital. 25 cents.

Yorktown (Virginia). Describes one of the most momentous events in American history. 25 cents.

Manassas (Bull Run) (Virginia). Presents the history of two of the more famous battles of the Civil War, the First Battle of Manassas, July 21, 1861, and the Second Battle of Manassas, fought approximately a year later, which paved the way for Lee's first invasion of the North. 25 cents.

Fort Raleigh (North Carolina). Tells the story of the Lost Colony. 25 cents.

Independence (Pennsylvania). Describes Independence Hall and the signing of the Declaration of Independence. 25 cents.

Fort Pulaski (Georgia). The age-old struggle between offense and defense is the principal story of Fort Pulaski. Giving numerous details about the construction of the fort, this pamphlet also reveals many dramatic events which led to its siege and surrender. 25 cents.

Fort Necessity (Pennsylvania). Describes the action at Fort Necessity during the French and Indian War in colonial America. 25 cents.

Fort Laramie (Wyoming). A story of the Indian Wars in the West. 25 cents.

Vicksburg (Mississippi). Gives the history of the campaign and siege at Vicksburg, the last Confederate stronghold on the Mississippi River, in June, 1863. 25 cents.

King's Mountain (South Carolina). The southern campaign of the American Revolution. 25 cents.

Bandelier (New Mexico). Preserves the ruined dwellings of the most extensive prehistoric Indian populations of the historical Southwest. 25 cents.

Ocmulgee (Georgia). Describes one of the first large Indian sites in the South to be scientifically excavated. 25 cents.

Chicamauga and Chattanooga Battlefields (Georgia-Tennessee). Relates the Battle of Chickamauga and the struggle for control of Chattanooga, the gateway through the mountains to the heart of the Confederacy. 25 cents.

George Washington Birthplace (Virginia). The story of the Washington family plantation in Westmoreland County, Virginia. 25 cents.

Montezuma Castle (Arizona). Describes the pueblo ruins in the Verde River Valley of central Arizona. 25 cents.

Scotts Bluff (Nebraska). Tells the story of this celebrated landmark on the great North Platte Valley trunk line of "the Oregon Trail." 30 cents.

Chalmete (Louisiana). Site of the Battle of New Orleans, the last big battle and the greatest American land victory of the War of 1812. 25 cents.

Guilford Courthouse (North Carolina). Describes a battle which marked the beginning of the end of the Revolutionary struggle. 25 cents.

Antietam (Maryland). Described in this pamphlet are the interesting events leading to the violent conflict of two great armies, colliding almost by chance, which shattered the quiet of Maryland's countryside on September 18, 1862—the bloodiest day of the Civil War. 25 cents.

Vanderbilt Mansion National Historic Site (New

York). Presents the history of the Vanderbilt Mansion and the Vanderbilt family, with a detailed, illustrated description of the mansion and its grounds. 25 cents.

Richmond Battlefields (Virginia). Briefly describes some of the events and battles that took place in the vicinity of the Confederate capital. 25 cents.

Wright Brothers National Memorial (North Carolina). Tells the story of Wilbur and Orville Wright and their successful flight at Kitty Hawk and gives a brief description of the points of interest at the Memorial. 30 cents.

Fort Union National Monument (New Mexico). This pamphlet, well illustrated with pictures, photographs, drawings, and maps, relates the story of the founding of Fort Union in 1851, the part the fort played as guardian of the Santa Fe Trail, and its participation in the Apache War, the Ute War, the Civil War, and other campaigns, until its abandonment in 1891. 30 cents.

Aztec Ruins National Monument (New Mexico). This historical handbook tells the story of the men in the San Juan Valley—early hunters and gatherers, the Basketmakers, the Pueblos, and the Aztec Pueblo. It describes the exploration and excavations of these well-preserved ruins, as well as the ruins as they are today. 30 cents.

And for more recent history, you can refer to a new edition of the *Public Papers of John F. Kennedy*. Here you'll read verbatim transcripts of the President's speeches, news conferences, messages to Congress, and other materials. The book is $9.00 and is the latest edition in a series of Papers of the Presidents of the United States.

And history is not restricted to words, either. For $2.50 you can order a set of fourteen full-color reproductions depicting heroic exploits of American fighting men. These are reproductions of paintings hanging in the Pentagon—paintings that graphically depict scenes of heroism and courage by American fighting men in every war in which this nation has been involved, from the American Revolution to the action in Korea. They provide an inspiring gallery of art that vividly reminds us why America has remained a free nation since we declared our independence 188 years ago. Each picture contains a brief description of the action portrayed. Titles are:

Merry Christmas, 1776. Trenton, New Jersey, December 26, 1776. At dawn General Washington's artillery opened a surprise attack at Trenton. This victory over superior forces was a turning point in the war.

The Road to Fallen Timbers. Ohio, August 20, 1794. Tracking down the Indians of the Northwest who had twice whipped our Army, the Legion met with the foe on the banks of the Maumee, Ohio, routed him from behind a vast windfall, and destroyed his warriors.

"Those Are Regulars, By God!" Chippewa, Upper Canada, July 5, 1814. As the American troops advanced steadily through murderous grapeshot, the British commander opposing them realized his mistake in believing them to be the untrained levies he had easily whipped before. In this battle at Chippewa, Upper Canada, this crack brigade of United States infantry drove the British from the battlefield.

"Remember Your Regiment." Resaca de la Palma, Texas, May 9, 1846. In an attack that climaxed the opening campaign of the Mexican War, a squadron

of the Second Dragoons slashed through the enemy lines.

First at Vicksburg. Confederate Lines, Vicksburg, Mississippi, May 19, 1863. The First Battalion of the Thirteenth Infantry lost 43 per cent of its men in this bitter battle during which the soldiers of both sides demonstrated their bravery in hand-to-hand combat.

Good Marksmanship and Guts. Near Fort Kearney, Wyoming, August 2, 1867. Thirty men of the Ninth Infantry chose to stand and fight when attacked by some 2,000 Sioux Indians in the Wagon Box Fight near Fort Kearney. Suffering only three casualties in the fight, this small force killed and wounded several hundred Sioux.

Gatlings to the Assault. San Juan Hill, Santiago de Cuba, July 1, 1898. During the assault on San Juan Hill in the war with Spain, the Gatling Gun Detachment gave fire support to the attacking infantry. This, the U.S. Army's first use of close-support machineguns in the attack, was decisive in the capture of San Juan Hill.

"I'll Try Sir!" Boxer Rebellion, 1900. During the fiercely opposed relief expedition to Peking in the Boxer Rebellion, when two companies of the U.S. Army's Fourteenth Infantry Regiment were pinned down by heavy fire between abutments of the Chinese City Wall, a trumpeter from E Company volunteered to make the first perilous ascent of the wall.

Knocking Out the Moros. Philippines, June, 1913. In the four-day battle of Bagsak Mountain on Jolo Island, Americans of the Eighth Infantry and the Philippine Scouts brought to an end years of bitter struggle against the fierce Moro pirates.

"The Rock of the Marne." Near Mezy, France, July, 1918. In their first taste of combat, the Thirtieth and Thirty-eighth Infantry Regiments of the Third

Division kept the crack troops of the German Army out of Paris in the historic Battle of the Marne.

Raid on Ploesti. May 31, 1944. B-24's of the Fifteenth Air Force attacking the refineries at Ploesti, an important source of petroleum products for the Nazi war machine. These raids on strategic Nazi industries curtailed production and forced the Nazi government into a costly program of industrial maintenance, reconstruction, and rebuilding underground.

"Follow Me!" Leyte, October 20, 1944. In the face of heavy machine-gun and rifle fire from Japanese pillboxes on Red Beach, the leading elements of the Third Battalion, Thirty-fourth Infantry, U.S. Army, were led forward by the Regimental Commander and succeeded in establishing a beachhead on Leyte.

Remagen Bridgehead. March 7, 1945. Although the Ludendorff Bridge crossing the Rhine at Remagen was mined for demolition and its destruction was imminent, the men of the Ninth Armored Division rushed across the structure without hesitation and seized the surrounding high ground. This, the first bridgehead across Germany's formidable river barrier, contributed decisively to the defeat of the enemy.

Breakthrough at Chipyong-Ni. Korea, February, 1951. When the men of the Twenty-third Infantry were cut off from the Eighth Army and surrounded by Chinese Reds, an armored unit smashed through to save the trapped soldiers and their arms.

More than a million of these fine paintings have been sold since the government first put them on the market.

MORE HISTORY . . .

For $3.00 you can get the *Guide to Federal Archives Relating to the Civil War*, describing government records during the 1860's: 721 pages of solid, documented statements on the most interesting and bloody conflict of our history.

Or turn to *Image of America*, an illustrated catalogue of photographs taken from the early days of the art through the turn of the century, depicting various aspects of American life, history, and progress to about 1900. The catalogue contains 46 reproductions and describes more than 300 other photographs in various categories.

MAPS . . .

Did you know you can get an aerial view of your own home so clear that you can count the lilac bushes in the front yard? The Department of Agriculture supplies aerial photographs of any section of the United States (restricted areas excluded, of course) at $2.10 for one 18 by 22 inches or $5.50 for 40 by 40 inches. The large print is scaled at 400 feet to the inch. If you want a map of a western section, send to Western Laboratory, Performance Division, Commodity Stabilization Service, Department of Agriculture, 2505 Parlays Way, Salt Lake City 9, Utah. For an eastern map, send to Washington 25, D.C., as usual.

The Department of the Interior Geological Survey also offers topographic maps of any section of the country. These come in a number of scales and at various prices. Send to the Geological Survey, Washington 25, D.C., for more detailed description.

And if you feel like becoming a do-it-yourself-mapper, you can learn how through *Photogrammetric Mapping*, an engineering manual giving all the principles and procedures. Cost, 40 cents.

To help you with this stimulating hobby, you might go for a wall chart on the Metric System, for 50 cents, giving units and definitions, conversion tables, and even a recent change to a wave-length standard of length, as well as a section on temperature scales.

And before we leave the subject of maps, how would you like to know something about them? You can learn all about it through *Elements of Map Projection* ($2.75). This 220-page illustrated book tells you in simple language and diagram about the ideas behind map and chart construction. By the time you've gone through it, you'll not only have a more complete understanding of what it takes to make a map and a greater respect for the men who make them; you'll be able to construct a map yourself.

CHOW'S ON! . . .

Agriculture and HEW, through their consumer and home-economic services, publish many books on cooking —so many that I won't begin to try to list them here. One sample is *Family Fare* (35 cents), mentioned at the beginning of this chapter among the "top twenty-five" government best sellers. Another is *Tips on Cooking Fish and Shellfish* (10 cents). But you ought to know that Uncle Sam has experience in feeding his nephews not individually, but by the thousands, in the Armed Forces. And the series of Navy Recipe Service cards, listing taste-tempting recipes covering many varieties of dishes, should be ideally useful for institutions serving large groups. The cards come with index separators, ready to file. If this interests you, you can get Issue No. 7, the least expensive set of 58 recipes, for $1.00. If you like what you see, you can order the other Issues totaling over 800 recipes.

A FINAL WORD . . .

Well, there it is. Obviously, I could go on and on. Books on art, books on music . . . did you know that the Navy publishes a *Hymnal* and a book on music theory?

You can win many a bet by convincing your open-mouthed friends that they can't name a subject, from A to Z, from the cradle to the grave, from athlete's foot to space travel, on which Uncle Sam hasn't published some useful information!

How can any American survey this treasure-trove without feeling a surge of love and pride, without voicing a silent prayer of humble thanks for the privilege of being part of a nation truly "of the people, by the people, and for the people."

BIBLIOGRAPHY

Department of Agriculture. Aerial photographs of any section of the United States except restricted areas. 18 by 22 inches, $2.10; 40 by 40 inches, $5.50.
————. *Cooperative Economic Insect Report.*
Department of the Interior Geological Survey (Washington 25, D.C.). *Photogrammetric Mapping.* 40 cents.
————. *Metric System.* 50 cents.
————. *Elements of Map Projection.* $2.75.
Superintendent of Documents. The "Top 25" government publications of the year, listed above in this chapter and priced from 10 cents to $2.50.

————. All the following categories and titles.
Basic Photography $2.00.
Handbook for Photo Lab Processing. $4.75.
Installation and Maintenance of Aerial Photo-
    graphic Equipment, Air Force Manual 95-3.
    $3.00.
Method for Determining Resolving Power of
    Photographic Lenses. $1.75.
Military Standardization Handbook, Glossary of
    Photographic Terms. 70 cents.
Photographer's Mate 2. $2.25.
Photographer's Mate 3. $3.00.
Photographer's Mate 1 & C. $2.25.
Electric Current Abroad. 25 cents.

Attracting Birds. 15 cents.
Backpacking in the National Forest Wilderness.
    15 cents.
Ducks at a Distance. 25 cents.
Hamster Raising. 5 cents.
Harbor Craft Crewman's Handbook. $1.50.
Migration of Birds. 35 cents.
The National Watercraft Collection. $3.50.
Raising Rabbits. 20 cents.
Recreational Boating Guide. 40 cents.
Weather Forecasting. 25 cents.

Charters of Freedom (facsimiles):
    The Bill of Rights. 45 cents.
    The Constitution of the United States. 45 cents.
    The Declaration of Independence. 45 cents.
    Set of all three $1.35.

Electronics, Electricity, Radar, and Radio: various
    titles priced from 10 cents to $2.75.

14 Full-Color Reproductions Depicting Heroic Exploits of American Fighting Men. 20 by 24 inches, suitable for framing. $2.50 per set.

Guide to Federal Archives Relating to the Civil War. $3.00.
Image of America.

Historical Handbook Series (Catalogue No. I 29.58). 36 booklets, ranging in price from 20 cents to 30 cents.
Public Papers of John F. Kennedy. $9.00.

Yearbooks of Agriculture. From $2.00 to $2.75.

CHAPTER XI

UNCLE AS YOUR INFORMATION FINDER

For today's businessmen seeking commercial information on firms in the United States, a variety of sources are available through libraries and private organizations.

Recently the Commercial Intelligence Division of the Office of International Trade Promotion, Bureau of International Commerce, made up a list of many sources from which names, addresses, and commercial information on business firms in the United States and in its noncontiguous areas are available. Handbooks giving more detailed references also are described. The directories included are, in the main, limited to those which are revised periodically or kept up to date with supplements. Current prices are shown in most cases, but are subject to change as new editions are published.

SOURCES OF INFORMATION ON AMERICAN FIRMS FOR INTERNATIONAL BUYERS

As the U.S. Department of Commerce does not compile for distribution lists of firms in the United States or data on their individual operations, this directory has been prepared by the Commercial Intelligence Division to serve as a guide in obtaining such information.

Identified here are some of the many sources from which names, addresses, and commercial information on business firms in the United States and in its noncontiguous areas are available. Handbooks giving more detailed references also are described. The directories included are, in the main, limited to those which are revised periodically or kept up to date with supplements.

The Department of Commerce does maintain series of Trade Lists of foreign firms, grouped under about 75 commodity classifications and compiled by individual countries; the charge is $1 for each list covering one country and classification. Also, among the Trade Lists is a series covering American Firms, Subsidiaries, and Affiliates in individual foreign countries (see Business Directories section of this directory.

The Department also provides World Trade Directory (WTD) reports, at $1 each, furnishing business information on specific foreign firms.

Descriptions and samples of Trade Lists and WTD reports are contained in a leaflet, Low-Cost Marketing Aids for Higher Export Profits. Available on request from the Commercial Intelligence Division, Bureau of International Commerce, U.S. Department of Commerce, Washington, D.C. 20230, or any of the Department's Field Offices.

LOCAL SOURCES

PUBLIC LIBRARIES

A basic method of finding business information is through use of the facilities of the public library system. Public libraries have standard reference guides, commercial and industrial directories, financial reference manuals such as those named on the following pages, and other data of value to the businessman.

Many of the larger libraries have established specialized and comprehensive business reference collections which include guides to business research, trade journals, Government publications (Federal, State, and municipal), and lists of books, booklets, and articles on business subjects.

Described below is an example of the general reference publications which provide guidance to those interested in business research.

BASIC LIBRARY REFERENCE SOURCES FOR BUSINESS USE.
Small Business Bibliography No. 18.

A pamphlet designed to simplify library research by listing and describing briefly selected catalogs, manuals, and guides to sources of business information. Single copies available on request from U.S. Small Business Administration, Washington, D.C. 20416, and its Field Offices.

Trained librarians can quickly direct the inquirer to appropriate reference sources. When the library is unable to supply needed information, the experienced librarian may know where it can be found in the community or make inquiry by letter or telephone to likely sources. The national interlibrary loan system is often utilized to obtain material for the researcher.

Business information also is frequently available in municipal reference libraries, as well as those maintained by city and State agencies, research and trade organizations, large corporations, or schools and colleges. The location of the various kinds of libraries in a particular region or community can be found in the following publication, available at most public libraries:

AMERICAN LIBRARY DIRECTORY,
R. R. Bowker Co., 1180 Avenue of the Americas, New York, N. Y. 10018. Published biennially. $25.

Lists, by State and city, libraries in the United States and Canada. Covers libraries in U.S. noncontiguous areas —Canal Zone, Guam, Puerto Rico, Virgin Islands.

Lists Government libraries, libraries operated by private organizations, college and university libraries, and special libraries. Indicates U.S. document depository libraries.

CHAMBERS OF COMMERCE

The local chamber of commerce is often one of the best sources of information concerning trade and industry in the area. Larger organizations will generally have city directories, general directories, or other specialized references, as well as trade journals covering industries of importance in the region. In many large communities, chambers of commerce publish classified buyers' guides, manufacturers' guides, or lists of international traders in their localities. Chamber of commerce executives and staff members are well informed on business in the area and are in a position to give sound advice and make helpful recommendations to the inquirer.

Listings of chambers of commerce are included in some of the directories and guides described elsewhere in this pamphlet.

CITY DIRECTORIES

In many communities city directories are published annually or biennially by commercial firms, although such directories are no longer published for some of the largest cities because publication costs exceed revenue from sales and advertising. A standard city directory includes a classified listing of business firms. Because of widespread demand, collections of city directories have been established in many cities of the United States, such collections may be found in public libraries, chambers of commerce, or the offices of local directory publishers.

Information on city directories is contained in the publication cited below, copies of which may be consulted in libraries or purchased from the publisher.

CATALOG OF CITY, COUNTY, AND STATE DIRECTORIES PUBLISHED IN NORTH AMERICA.

Association of North American Directory Publishers, 60 E. 56th Street, New York, N. Y., 10022. Annual. $1.

Lists directories alphabetically by States and cities, keyed to indicate publishers.

TELEPHONE DIRECTORIES

The "buyer's guide" nearest at hand is the classified section of the telephone directory which lists firms and individuals by line of business or service.

Out-of-town directories frequently are available for

reference in public libraries or in the office of the local telephone company, or they may be purchased through the local telephone company. In cities of some size, copies of out-of-town directories often are found at large hotels, as well as at railway and bus terminals and airports.

BANKS AND CREDIT REPORTING AGENCIES

Reports on the financial or credit standing of U.S. firms are obtainable through local banks, mercantile reporting agencies, credit bureaus, and similar organizations, names of which are included in classified telephone directories. Specialized banking directories, giving detailed information on banks throughout the country, are listed in some of the guides named in the Directories of Directories section of this pamphlet.

The source described below is primarily a credit-rating service but is often used by subscribers as a directory because of its current and comprehensive listing of American enterprises. Financial ratings and information on the reliability of individual concerns also may be found in some of the other publications cited in this pamphlet.

REFERENCE BOOK OF DUN & BRADSTREET, INC.

Dun & Bradstreet, Inc., 99 Church Street, New York, N. Y., 10007. Revised bimonthly. Loaned under yearly subscription contract agreement.

Lists names and financial and credit ratings of manufacturers, wholesalers, and retailers in the United States, arranged by States and cities or towns, and keyed to indicate line of business according to Standard Industrial Classification code. Also shows year of establishment. Lists banks in each locality with amount of capital and principal officers.

Detailed credit reports on individual firms available to subscribers.

BUSINESS DIRECTORIES

Business directories published in the United States number in the thousands and vary markedly in size and character. They range from comprehensive general national directories of industrial firms, classified and cross-indexed in several volumes, to pocketsize local restaurant guides.

There are many special directories of particular industries, commodities, and profesions, as well as general directories covering individual States, regions, and cities. It is not the purpose of this book to list these more specialized directories but rather to provide examples of standard general directories which cover a major portion of all industries and trade, which are generally country-wide in scope, and which are usually available for reference in libraries, local chambers of commerce, and similar business organizations.

The following have been selected as representative of directories of this type. Many additional national and regional directories are to be found in the handbooks listed in the Directories of Directories section of this pamphlet.

MANUFACTURERS

Examples of national directories of manufacturers are described below:

THOMAS' REGISTER OF AMERICAN MANUFACTURERS.
Thomas Publishing Co., 461 Eighth Avenue, New York, N. Y., 10001. Annual $20.

Comprehensive directory in four volumes with separately bound finding guide to contents. Lists manufacturers, arranged geographically under product classifications, with street addresses and capital ratings; listed alphabetically with home office address, rating, indication of nature of products and of interest in export business, directing officials, branches, and subsidiaries; alphabetical trade name section.

MACRAE'S BLUE BOOK.
MacRae's Blue Book Co., 18 East Huron Street, Chicago, Ill. 60611. Annual. Classified section and address section. $20.

Purchasing reference directory in two volumes, giving sources of supply in the United States of industrial equipment, products, and materials. Classified materials section, main volume, is alphabetical arrangement of product classifications with manufacturers listed for each product. Separately bound address-trade-name section lists manufacturers alphabetically with home office address, principal products, and invested capital ratings; trade name and trademark identification.

CONOVER-MAST PURCHASING DIRECTORY.

Conover-Mast Purchasing Director, 205 E. 42d Street, New York, N. Y., 10017. Semiannual (spring and fall). Subscription price, $25 (free to executives in charge of purchasing activities).

Covers sources for plant equipment, supplies, and services used by industry. Designed to meet needs of production, purchasing, and engineering executives.

Contains five sections: A product classification section listing industrial products manufactured by U.S. companies with firm names and addresses; a chemical section; a mechanical data section devoted to mathematical tables and formulas; a trade-name section; and an address/telephone section.

SWEET'S CATALOG FILES.

Sweet's Catalog Service, division of F. W. Dodge Corp., 330 W. 42nd Street, New York, N. Y., 10036. Annual. Distribution begins in February. Rates obtainable from publisher.

Six classified bound files of manufacturers catalogs: Architectural Catalog File, Light Construction Catalog File, Industrial Construction Catalog File, Plant Engineering Catalog File, Metalworking Equipment Catalog File, and Product Design Catalog File.

Files provided for selected offices without charge. Copies are available for reference in major public, and appropriate school libraries. Firm names, products, and trade names indexed alphabetically. Data on markets, and information on catalog design, production, and distribution services available.

MANUFACTURERS' AGENTS' GUIDE.
Manufacturers' Agent Publishing Co., 554 Fifth Avenue, New York, N. Y., 10036. Biennial. $15.

Lists U.S. manufacturers who distribute products through manufacturers' agents, arranged on an industry basis. Includes name and address of manufacturer, principal products, estimated financial rating, name and title of sales executive. Details steps to follow in dealing with manufacturers, suggests commission scales for various products. Shows suggested manufacturers' and manufacturers' agents' contract forms.

MANUFACTURERS' AGENTS

Directories of manufacturers' agents serving particular industries are published by many trade papers and journals. Below are some general sources of information of this kind. A related publication is the *Manufacturers' Agents' Guide*, just listed.

MANUFACTURERS' AGENTS NATIONAL ASSOCIATION DIRECTORY OF MEMBERS.
Annual July issue of the magazine, *The Agent and Representative*. Manufacturers' Agents National Association, 626 N. Garfield Avenue, Alhambra, Calif. 91801.

Lists names and addresses of members of the association, by State and city, showing general lines handled by each member and territory covered. Single copies free to manufacturers and suppliers.

**VERIFIED DIRECTORY OF MANUFACTURERS' REPRESENTA-
TIVES (AGENTS).**

Manufacturers' Agent Publishing Co., 554 Fifth Avenue, New York, N. Y., 10036. Biennial. $20.

Roster of manufacturers' domestic and export representatives in the United States, Puerto Rico, and Canada. Listings, arranged by States and cities, include principal product line carried and territory covered.

Introductory section tabulates typical commission rates for various product classifications, gives pointers on drawing up sales contracts, and describes factors conducive to good working arrangement. Includes suggested manufacturer's and manufacturer's agent's contract forms.

EXPORTERS AND IMPORTERS

As the number of national directories of exporters and importers is limited, references to a representative local directory is included here. Trade journals published in the United States often contain information on firms in specialized fields which engage in international trade. An example of a general listing compiled by a trade publication is also included in the following group. The classified sections of most large city telephone directories list importers and exporters in the locality.

Over 100 local chambers of commerce in the United States maintain departments, bureaus, or committees of foreign trade and many have compiled lists of importers and exporters in their areas. These chambers will gladly reply to inquiries; in some instances, the lists are available without charge. Chambers which maintain foreign trade facilities are identified in the *Foreign Commerce Handbook*, published by the Chamber of Commerce of the United States, 1615 H Street NW., Washington, D.C., 20006. $2.

AMERICAN EXPORTER ANNUAL BUYERS GUIDE TO EXPORT PRODUCTS.

Included in January issue of American Exporter magazine. Johnston International Publishing Corporation, 386 Park Avenue S., New York, N. Y., 10016. Separately bound. $5.

A directory of products sold in international markets by manufacturers who advertise in Johnston International publications.

AMERICAN REGISTER OF EXPORTERS AND IMPORTERS.

American Register of Exporters and Importers Corp., 90 W. Broadway, New York, N. Y., 10007. Annual. $15.

U.S. firms actively interested in international trade listed under product classifications. Gives firm name and address with indication of products exported or imported.

Includes section listing combination export managers with code indicating lines handled; foreign buying agencies in the United States, steamship and air lines, firms financing foreign trade, world-trade banks, money exchanges, export packers, and freight forwarders.

Product indexes in English, Spanish, French and German.

DIRECTORY OF NEW YORK IMPORTERS.
Commerce and Industry Association Institute, Inc., 99 Church Street, New York, N. Y., 10007. $7.50.

Lists firms alphabetically. Gives date of establishment, bank reference, products imported, special brands handled, and principal countries from which products are imported. Commodity section catalogs products imported with cross index of foreign products.

DIRECTORY OF COMBINATION EXPORT MANAGERS.
Office of Small Business, Agency for International Development, U.S. Department of State.

Gives names and addresses of combination export managers, names and addresses of their clients, lines handled, and areas of operation. Divided into five separate commodity group sections: Section I, *Food, Feed* and *Fertilizer*, 40 cents; section II, *Fuel*, 25 cents; section III, *Raw Materials* and *Semi-finished Products*, 75 cents; section IV, *Machinery and Vehicles*, $1; section V, *Miscellaneous and Unclassified* $1. Available from Superintendent of Documents, U.S. Government Printing Office, Washington, D.C., 20402.

RETAILERS AND WHOLESALERS

Directories of retailers, buyers, and distributors in almost every line are published annually by trade journals, trade associations, and private firms. Following are examples of such directories published by private firms:

FAIRCHILD'S FINANCIAL MANUAL OF RETAIL STORES.

Fairchild Publications, Inc., 7 E. 12th Street, New York, N. Y., 10003. Annual. $15.

Contains financial information on major publicly owned retail organizations in the following categories: Department stores, specialty stores, home furnishings stores, variety stores, mail order concerns, drugstores, jewelry stores, shoe chains, closed-membership discount department stores, and food chains.

Shows address, officers, directors, branches; gives data on capital, surplus, income before taxes, earnings; 2-year comparisons of net sales and profits.

SHELDON'S RETAIL TRADE.

Phelon-Sheldon Publications, Inc., 32 Union Square, New York, N. Y., 10003. Annual. $20, including mid-year supplement-listing buyer changes.

Gives buying headquarters addresses of large independent department stores, junior department store chains, independent women's specialty stores, women's specialty store chains, independent and chain home-furnishing stores. Shows, for each firm, location of branches, general and divisional merchandise managers, and department buyers.

DIRECTORY OF DISCOUNT HOUSES AND SELF-SERVICE DEPARTMENT STORES, 1962.

National Research Bureau, Inc., 415 Dearborn Street, National Research Bureau, Inc., 221 N. LaSalle Street, Chicago, Ill., 60601. $40. Iincludes 12 monthly supplements.

Data on discount and self-service stores (chain and independent). In geographical arrangement, gives name of company, headquarters address, and such details as number and location of stores operated, sales volume, parking facilities, type of operation, phone number, date store opened, size, lines carried, leased departments, store hours, store manager, and merchandise buyers. Alphabetical index.

DIRECTORY OF SHOPPING CENTERS IN UNITED STATES AND CANADA, 1962.

Bureau, Inc., 221 N. LaSalle Street, Chicago, Ill., 60601. $40. Includes 12 monthly supplements.

By States and cities, gives data on shopping centers, including name of center, address, owner/developer, manager, leasing agent, size and cost of physical plant, date opened, availability of rental space, and names of tenant stores.

Lists centers planned, under construction, and for which complete information is unavailable; key personnel connected with shopping centers; leading national chain store tenants, by merchandising field; and shopping centers by largest Standard Metropolitan Areas.

PHELON'S DISCOUNT DEPARTMENT STORES.
  Phelon-Sheldon Publications, Inc., 32 Union Square, New York, N. Y., 10003. Annual. $20

  Contains infomation on discount stores and discount chains, most of which handle complete line of department store merchandise, soft and hard. Shows buying head-quarters and, in many instances, executives, lines of mer-chandise bought, buyers, leased departments, lessees, num-ber of stores and price range.

PHELON'S RETAIL EXECUTIVES.
  Phelon-Sheldon Publications, Inc., 32 Union Square, New York, N. Y., 10003. Annual. $25.

  Directory of major executives of the larger department and chain department stores. Lists stores with number of outlets operated, president, general manager, and managers in charge of sales promotion, display, advertising or pub-licity, and real estate; also store supply buyer.

  Midyear supplement, listing changes in executives, included in price.

PHELON'S RESIDENT BUYERS BOOK AND MERCHANDISE BROKERS OF DEPARTMENT STORE MERCHANDISE, READY TO WEAR, MILLINERY.
  Phelon-Sheldon Publications, Inc., 32 Union Square, New York, N. Y., 10003. Annual. $10.

  Lists New York City buying offices, resident buyers, merchandise brokers, chain headquarters, and offices in Chicago and Los Angeles. Includes phone numbers, type of goods purchased, and firms for which each office buys. Contains alphabetical list of out-of-town firms and location of their New York, Chicago, and Los Angeles offices.

SHELDON'S JOBBING AND WHOLESALE TRADE.
Phelon-Sheldon Publications, Inc., 32 Union Square, New York, N. Y., 10003. Biennial $12.

Lists jobbing firms, including rack jobbers, dealing in piece goods, notions, knit goods, men's furnishings, stationery, underwear, women's-children's infants' wear, toys, and housewares. Shows class of merchandise bought by each firm, buyers' names, and address of New York office.

ADVERTISERS, ADVERTISING AND MARKETING RESEARCH AGENCIES

The first directory included in the following group identifies business firms in various fields as well as advertising agencies.

Directories of advertising media are described in the Trade Journals section of this directory.

STANDARD DIRECTORY OF ADVERTISERS.
National Register Publishing Co., Inc., 147 W. 42d Street, New York, N.Y., 10036. Classified and geographical editions published annually with monthly revision supplements. $65 a year for either service; $100 a year including 3 issues of the Agency List described in the next entry.

Lists national advertisers grouped according to product classifications. Includes name and address of company, executive personnel, products, advertising agency handling the account, and the media used.

STANDARD DIRECTORY OF ADVERTISING AGENCIES.
National Register Publishing Co., Inc., 147 W. 42d Street, New York, N. Y., 10036. Published in January, May, and September. $35 a year.

Lists advertising agencies with their personnel and accounts.

AMERICAN ASSOCIATION OF ADVERTISING AGENCIES— A.A.A.A. ROSTER AND ORGANIZATION.
American Association of Advertising Agencies, 200 Park Avenue, New York, N. Y., 10017. Annual.

Alphabetical listing of member agencies, operating offices in the United States and abroad; gives home office address, location of branches. Listed geographically, by State and city; also by foreign country. Includes committees and regional councils. Single copies available to firms and organizations by request on letterhead.

BRADFORD'S DIRECTORY OF MARKETING RESEARCH AGENCIES IN THE UNITED STATES AND FOREIGN COUNTRIES.
Bradford's Directory of Marketing Research Agencies, P.O. Box 207, Middleburg, Va., 22117. Biennial. $15 for billing; $13.50 for each cash order.

Geographical arrangement of marketing research and management firms in United States and foreign countries. For each organization, gives description of services, date established, principal officers, size of staff, location of branch offices. Alphabetical list of firms.

GEOGRAPHIC LISTING OF MARKETING CONSULTING AND RESEARCH AGENCIES.

American Marketing Association, 230 N. Michigan Avenue, Chicago, Ill., 60611. $2 to nonmembers.

Designed as aid to business firms attempting to locate marketing research assistance. Lists only those firms and their branches which have at least one member of the firm in the American Marketing Association. Arrangement by State and city showing company address, principal officer, coded information as to specialty of firm and extent of services, date of establishment. Branch offices listed under appropriate city, with parent company indicated. Similar data for certain foreign countries. Alphabetical index of companies.

INVESTMENT REFERENCE SERVICES

Investment reference manuals, intended as sources of financial data for buyers and sellers of securities, may also be used as directories since they provide information on type of business and product, subsidiaries, plant locations, and officials of companies which they list.

MOODY'S INDUSTRIAL MANUAL.

Moody's Investor Service, 99 Church Street, New York, N. Y., 10007. Annual (July) volume with twice-weekly loosleaf bulletins.

One of five manuals published yearly by this service. Contains detailed descriptions of industrial companies in the United States and major foreign countries. Listings include summary of firm's interests and operation, principal plants and subsidiaries, officers and directors, comparative income accounts, long-term record of earnings, and other financial and operating data.

Other Moody Manuals cover the fields of Banks and Finance, Public Utilities, Government and Municipals, and Transportation. Available on lease basis. Subscription rates obtainable from publisher.

STANDARD & POOR'S CORPORATION RECORDS SERVICE.

Standard & Poor's Corporation, 345 Hudson Street, New York, N. Y., 10014. Annual. Six looseleaf volumes arranged alphabetically according to company, and fully indeed; kept up to date by monthly revisions and daily supplements. Subscription rates obtainable from publisher.

Provides factual information on major American and Canadian corporations and important developments affecting smaller concerns.

FITCH INVESTORS SERVICE.

120 Wall Street, New York, N. Y., 10005.

Monthly record on leading corporations whose securities are traded in the unlisted markets. Includes earnings, dividend record, quotations, nature of business, capitalization, and ratings. Price information available from publisher.

FIRST SELECTED BY SIZE

Following are examples of directories featuring data on the larger American firms. Some directories of this type rank the firms according to such factors as sales, assets, profits, and employment.

DUN & BRADSTREET MILLION DOLLAR DIRECTORY.
Dun & Bradstreet, Inc., 99 Church Street, New York, N. Y., 10007. Annual; supplements issued twice yearly. Available on lease basis only, $98.50 a year; renewals, $84.50.

Lists business enterprises in the United States with an indicated worth of a million dollars and over. Section I names firms alphabetically, State where incorporated, address, principal products or service, Standard Industrial Classification (SIC) code number, annual sales, number of employees, names and titles of directing personnel.

Section II is geographical arrangement of firms by State and city. Section III indexes firms by SIC product classification. Section IV lists officers, directors, and other principals alphabetically with their titles and names and addresses of companies with which affiliated.

DUN & BRADSTREET MIDDLE MARKET DIRECTORY.
Dun & Bradstreet, Inc., 99 Church Street, New York, N. Y., 10007. Annual. Available on lease basis, $98.50 a year; renewals, $84.50.

Covers business enterprises in the United States with an indicated worth of $500,000 to $999,999. Contains three sections listing businesses alphabetically, geographically, and by Standard Industrial Classification (SIC) product codes.

The alphabetical section includes for each firm the State of incorporation, headquarters address, line of business, SIC codes, annual sales, number of employees, and names and titles of principal officers.

FORTUNE PLANT AND PRODUCT DIRECTORY OF THE 1,000 LARGEST U.S. INDUSTRIAL CORPORATIONS.
Fortune, Time & Life Bldg., New York, N. Y., 10020. Annual. $90.

Directory of all the manufacturing plants and all the products of the 1,000 largest U.S. industrial companies. First of three sections lists companies alphabetically with headquarters address, figures on sales, assets, profits and employment for the fiscal year, and for each of such figures showing numerical rank of company among the 1,000, also lists products by 5-digit Standard Industrial Classification (SIC) code, and plant locations.

Second section lists plants geographically, shows, for each, products and number of employees. Product classification section gives SIC numbers, companies manufacturing each product, and cities and States where each product is made.

A Directory of the 500 Largest U.S. Industrial Corporations also is published annually in *Fortune Magazine*. It ranks companies by sales with comparisons for the previous year. Single reprint, 50¢.

U.S. FIRMS IN FOREIGN COUNTRIES

Financial reference manuals and other guides supply information on foreign subsidiaries and affiliates of U.S. firms. An additional source is the Trade List series:

AMERICAN FIRMS, SUBSIDIARIES, AND AFFILIATES IN— (foreign country).

U.S. Department of Commerce, Washington, D.C., 20230. $1 each.

A series of Trade Lists, available for approximately 70 individual countries, compiled by the U.S. Foreign Service. Entries show name and address of local firm, description of its business activity, and name and address of affiliated or parent organization in the United States.

The lists include only those concerns in which American firms or individuals have a substantial direct capital investment in the form of stock, as the sole owner, or as a partner in the enterprise.

Available from the Commerce Department's Commercial Intelligence Division, Bureau of International Commerce, or from any of the Department's Field Offices. Requests should specify country.

DIRECTORS AND EXECUTIVES

Among the primary sources of biographic information on American businessmen are the two specialized directories cited below. Also, many business and professional

men are listed in *Who's Who in America* and other biographical dictionaries.

Many biographical publications covering more limited
geographic areas or fields of operation, are listed in some
of the guides named in the Directories of Directories section of this pamphlet.

**POOR'S REGISTER OF CORPORATIONS, DIRECTORS AND
EXECUTIVES**

Standard & Poor's Corp., 345 Hudson Street, New
York, N. Y., 10014. Annual: January. Cumulative supplements issued April, July, and November. $100;
available on lease basis at $84 a year.

Arranged in two principal parts. First in alphabetical
list of leading American and Canadian corporations giving
home office, number of employees, approximate annual
sales, principal products with Standard Industrial Classification (SIC) numbers for these products, and directors.
Classified index lists these companies according to industry
classifications, arranged by SIC numbers.

Second major section gives brief descriptions of individual officers of the listed corporations.

WORLD WHO'S WHO IN COMMERCE AND INDUSTRY.

Marquis-Who's Who Incorporated, Marquis Publications Building, 210 E. Ohio Street, Chicago, Ill.,
60611. $26.

Contains alphabetically arranged summaries of background and affiliations of ranking business executives and
others in commerce and industry in the United States and
other countries of the free world.

Includes alphabetical index of selected principal firms in the countries covered. Provides business-to-executive reference by index keys that link these companies to biographical data on their chief executives.

MAILING LIST HOUSES

The names and addresses of companies which prepare and sell mailing lists may be found in the classified sections of telephone directories under such headings as Lists, Mailing Lists, or Addressing and Letter Services. Some mailing list houses offer direct mail service, including such operations as addressing, folding, inserting, stamping, and mailing; also duplicating services, sales letters, circulars, and other promotional material.

Names and addresses of many companies compiling mailing lists, and descriptions of the lists which they offer, are given in the following national guides:

DIRECTORY OF MAILING LIST HOUSES,
B. Klein & Co., 27 E. 22d Street, New York, N. Y., 10010. $15.

Guide to mailing list houses in the United States, arranged geographically. Shows name, address, name of manager, year organized (when information is available), types of lists handled, and mailing services offered.

NATIONAL MAILING LIST HOUSES.
Small Business Bibliography No. 29.

Directory of compilers and brokers of mailing lists of national scope. Designed for distributors of goods and services, letter shops, and others who want to buy or sell mailing lists. Catalogs general-line houses, with indication as to nature of each firm's business, and number of lists offered.

Alphabetical arrangement of limited-line houses with indication of principal types of lists in which they specialize.

Single copies available free from the U.S. Small Business Administration, Washington, D.C., 20416, and its Field Offices.

LITERARY MARKET PLACE—BUSINESS DIRECTORY OF AMERICAN BOOK PUBLISHING,

R. R. Bowker Co., 1180 Avenue of the Americas, New York, N. Y., 10036. Annual. $7.45.

Handbook for those concerned with publishing, the book trade, and writers. Contains register of direct mail and promotion facilities, including names of mailing list brokers.

TRADE AND PROFESSIONAL ASSOCIATIONS

Directories are not available for some trades or industries; in these instances membership lists of trade associations, both national and local, are often useful.

Business and professional organizations are identified in the following directory. Names of commercial organizations also are found in the classified sections of telephone directories and are frequently included in general and specialized business directories.

ENCYCLOPEDIA OF ASSOCIATIONS.
Gale Research Co., 2200 Book Tower, Detroit, Mich. 48226. Vol. I, $25; Vol. II, $15.

Two-volume guide to nonprofit associations and similar organizations, primarily of national scope, in various fields.

Vol. I, National Organizations of the United States, lists organizations, according to basic types such as trade, business and commerce groups; chambers of commerce; public affairs organizations; and scientific, engineering, and technical associations. Gives name, headquarters address, year founded, name and title of managing official, number of members and staff, official publication. Alphabetical and key word index.

Vol. II, Geographic and Executive Index, presents organizations by State and city, with address and managing official of each.

TRADE JOURNALS

A number of companies which publish trade magazines also publish directories of concerns in the industry. These directories sometimes are contained in special issues of the magazines and are included in the subscription prices; in other instances they may be purchased separately.

The following sources contain the names and addresses of trade journals and their publishers. Most public libraries or offices of newspaper publishers have one or more of these volumes.

N. W. AYER & SON'S DIRECTORY OF NEWSPAPERS AND PERIODICALS,
N. W. Ayer & Son, Inc., West Washington Square, Philadelphia, Pa. 19106. Annual. $30.

Comprehensive roster of newspapers and periodicals of all kinds published in the United States and its non-contiguous areas, also Canada, Panama, Bermuda, and the Philippines. Main section arranged by State and city. Each entry includes data on size, circulation, advertising rates, frequency, and subscription price. Index to trade journals is contained in the classified section.

STANDARD RATE AND DATA SERVICE: BUSINESS PUBLICATION RATES AND DATA.
Standard Rate & Data Service, Inc., 5201 Old Orchard Road, Skokie, Ill., 60078. Monthly. $35 a year.

One section covers a periodical advertising rate service. Other sections cover newspapers, consumer magazines and farm publications, spot radio, spot television, films for television, network, and Canadian media (monthly); and transit advertising (quarterly).

Business Publication Rates and Data lists publications grouped under market classifications, including all regularly issued trade journals published in the United States. Each listing shows circulation, advertising rates, subscription price. Includes information on directory and buyers' guide issues of some of the periodicals listed and alphabetical indexes to publications and market classifications.

ULRICH'S PERIODICALS DIRECTORY.
> R. R. Bowker, 1180 Avenue of the Americas, New York, N. Y., 10036. Published triennially. $22.50.

A classified guide to foreign and domestic periodicals, arranged under subject headings. Includes publisher, price, frequency, whether indexed or abstracted and where, and date of founding. Index and key to titles and subjects.

ATP PERIODICALS DIRECTORY.
> American Trade Press Clipping Bureau, 15 E. 26th Street, New York, N. Y., 10010. Spiral bound. $12; including all supplements issued until new edition is published.

Under subjects categories, lists selected periodicals read regularly by the ATP. Gives name of periodical, address, and frequency of issue. Included are business, consumer, farm, labor, and other specialized publications. Contains index of subject categories, alphabetical index of periodicals.

SOURCES FOR NONCONTIGUOUS AREAS OF THE UNITED STATES

Data on firms and individuals in the noncontiguous areas of the United States are available from a number of sources already listed. This section identifies directories and information agencies which provide special coverage of these areas.

DIRECTORIES AND GUIDES

GUAM BUSINESS DIRECTORY.
Department of Commerce, Government of Guam, P.O. Box 1445, Agana, Guam. Annual. Pocketsize.

Lists names and addresses of Guam retailers, wholesalers, service establishments, and professional people, classified by type of business or service.

DIRECTORY OF EDA MANUFACTURING PLANTS.
Economic Development Administration, Commonwealth of Puerto Rico, San Juan, Puerto Rico. Supplements quarterly.

A list of the names, addresses, products, employment, size, and names and addresses of mainland or foreign affiliates of Puerto Rican manufacturing enterprises which have been given various types of assistance by the Economic Development Administration or the Puerto Rico Industrial Development Company.

MANUFACTURING ESTABLISHMENTS IN PUERTO RICO.
Department of Labor, Bureau of Labor Statistics. Commonwealth of Puerto Rico, San Juan, Puerto Rico.

A list by municipalities and, within each municipality, by major industry group, of manufacturing establishments as revealed in annual October canvass. Listed are name of establishment, name of owner or manager, and address.

TRADE LISTS OF BUSINESS ENTERPRISES IN PUERTO RICO.
Department of Commerce, Commonwealth of Puerto Rico, San Juan, Puerto Rico.

A series of individual lists covering importers, exporters, dealers, retailers, wholesalers.

PUERTO RICO INDUSTRIAL, COMMERCIAL, AND PROFESSIONAL DIRECTORY.
Insular Advertising and Publishers Corporation, KM. 5HM. 2 State Road No. 2, P.O. Box 10325, Caparra Heights, Puerto Rico, 00905. $15, including postage.

Text in Spanish and English. General information about Puerto Rico, economic data. Industrial section covers Fomento factories in Puerto Rico and their products, with headings in English and Spanish; commercial and professional sections, arranged by cities and towns, list retailers, wholesalers, and other business firms, and lawyers, agronomists, contractors, dentists, pharmacists, and physicians; factory representatives in Puerto Rico; engineers, architects, and surveyors.

PUERTO RICO TELEPHONE DIRECTORY.
Puerto Rico Telephone Co., P.O. Box 4275, San Juan, Puerto Rico, 00905.

Lists firms and individuals in metropolitan area of San Juan and the Island of Puerto Rico (two volumes).

RYUKYU TRADE DIRECTORY.

The Department of Economics, Government of the Ruykyu Islands, Naha, Okinawa, Ryukyu Islands.

Classified listings of Ryukyu exporters and importers, arranged in two sections. Commodity index for each section. Printed in English.

BLUE GUIDE.

Anuario Professional Commercial e Industrial de Puerto Rico e Islas Virgenes, P.O. Box 8776, Santurce, Puerto Rico, 00908. Annual.

Includes classified listings of business and industrial firms in Puerto Rico and the Virgin Islands. Text in Spanish and English.

DIRECTORY-VIRGIN ISLANDS TELEPHONE CORPORATION.

Virgin Islands Telephone Corporation, Charlotte Amalie, St. Thomas, Virgin Islands, 00801.

Telephone directory with alphabetical listing of names of firms and individuals. Also contains classified business section, indexed by kinds of business.

THE LATIN AMERICAN MARKET GUIDE.

Dun & Bradstreet, Inc., 99 Church Street, New York, N. Y., 10007. Annual. In two volumes, arranged by countries. Section I, Middle America; Section II, South America, $100 each or $155 for both sections. Availble to subscribers only on loan.

Middle America includes sections for Puerto Rico and for the Virgin Islands of the United States. Individual section for each country, arranged geographically by cities and towns, contains names and addresses of manufacturers, importers, wholesalers, retailers, commission agents, distributors and service organizations, with addresses, indication of kind of business, and capital and credit ratings.

For each locality, shows population, banks, nearest port. Map, general information, and detailed marketing data for each country.

Individual reports available on firms in these and all other noncontiguous areas of the United States.

PACIFIC ISLANDS BUSINESS DIRECTORY.

> Universal Business Directories, Ltd., P.O. Box 793, Kingston Street, Auckland, C.I., New Zealand, Biennial. $8.60.

Geographical arrangement, by island groups. Includes section for Eastern (American) Samoa giving general information (geography, history, population, trade) and list of firms in Pago Pago, Island of Tutuila, classified by kind of business.

THE WEST INDIES AND CARIBBEAN YEAR BOOK.

> Thomas Skinner & Co. (Publishers), Ltd., 111 Broadway, New York, N. Y., 10006. Annual. $14.

Contents arranged geographically, by countries. Includes individual sections for Puerto Rico and Virgin Islands. Section for each area contains map, general information, and trade data, and a listing of manufacturers, wholesalers, retailers, and service organizations, classified by products and services. Directory also contains list of banks, oil companies, steamship agents, and communication companies with offices in the Panama Canal Zone.

INFORMATION AGENCIES

COMMONWEALTH OF PUERTO RICO

Economic Development Administration, Commonwealth of Puerto Rico, Banco Popular Building, Stop 22, San Juan, Puerto Rico. Offices also at 666 Fifth Avenue, New York, N. Y., 10019; 79 W. Monroe Street, Chicago, Ill., 60603; 54555 Wilshire Boulevard, Los Angeles, Calif., 90036; Dupont Plaza Center, Miami, Fla., 33032; 607 Boylston Street, Boston, Mass., 02116; Transportation Building, Penn Center, Philadelphia, Pa. 19144.

Office of the Commonwealth of Puerto Rico, 2210 R Street, N.W., Washington, D. C., 20008.

Puerto Rico, Santurce 29, Puerto Rico, 00908.

Chamber of Commerce of Puerto Rico (Camara de Comercio de Puerto Rico), P.O. Box 3789, San Juan, Puerto Rico, 00904.

PACIFIC ISLANDS

American Samoa: The Governor of American Samoa, Pago Pago, American Samoa.

Guam: Director of Commerce, Government of Guam, P.O. Box 1445, Agana, Guam.

Ryukyu Islands: Economic Development Department, Offices of the High Commissioner of the Ryukyu Islands,

APO 331, San Francisco, California; Trade Section, Economic Department, Government of the Ryukyu Islands, Naha, Okinawa, Ryukyu Islands.

Trust Territory of the Pacific Islands (embracing the Marshall Islands, the Caroline Islands, and the Mariana Islands, with the exceptions of Guam): Chief, Division of Insular Affairs, Office of Territories, U.S. Department of the Interior, Washington, D.C., 20240; High Commissioner, Trust Territory of the Pacific Islands, Box 542, Agana, Guam.

THE VIRGIN ISLANDS OF THE UNITED STATES

Department of Commerce, Government of the Virgin Islands, P.O. Box 806, Charlotte Amalie, St. Thomas, Virgin Islands. Office also at Christiansted, St. Croix, Virgin Islands.

St. Croix Chamber of Commerce, Christiansted, St. Croix, Virgin Islands.

St. Thomas Chamber of Commerce, Box 324, St. Thomas, Virgin Islands.

Virgin Islands Government Tourist Information Office, 16 W. 49th Street, New York, N.Y., 10020.

DIRECTORIES OF DIRECTORIES

The reference sources described here are useful in locating directories of a particular industry or region, or of companies engaged in specific line of business.

BULLETIN OF THE PUBLIC AFFAIRS INFORMATION SERVICE.
Public Affairs Information Service, 11 W. 40th Street, New York, N. Y. 10018. Weekly and cumulated bulletins, $100 a year; annual cumulated bulletin, $25 a year.

A standard library service. Indexes, by subject, current material published in English.

Contains extensive listing of directories of all kinds from all over the world. Entries give title, price, publisher, and description of contents.

MARKETING INFORMATION GUIDE (formerly titled **Distribution Data Guide**).
Office of Marketing and Services, Business and Defense Services Administration, U.S. Department of Commerce, Washington, D.C., 20230. Monthly. $2 a year, including supplements; single copies, 15¢ each; supplements, 20¢ each.

Contains listings, with annotations, of currently available basic information, statistics, surveys, reports, and other published material, both Government and nongovernment, of significance to those engaged in marketing and distribution.

Includes descriptions of new general and specialized trade directories, national and regional.

Sold by Department of Commerce Field Offices and by the Superintendent of Documents, U.S. Government Printing Office, Washington, D. C., 20402.

TRADE DIRECTORIES OF THE WORLD.

Croner Publications, 211-03 Jamaica Avenue, Queens Village, N. Y. $15, including 1 year's supplements.

A looseleaf service, kept up to date by monthly amendments and supplements. Contains data on business directories covering trades in the United States and foreign countries.

GUIDE TO AMERICAN DIRECTORIES.

B. Klein & Co., 27 E. 22d Street, New York, N. Y., 10010. $25.

Describes, under subject headings, major general and specialized business directories of the United States. Section on foreign directories.

SOURCES OF STATE INFORMATION AND STATE INDUSTRIAL DIRECTORIES.

State Chamber of Commerce Department, Chamber of Commerce of the United States, 1615 H Street, N.W., Washington, D.C., 20006. Pocketsize, 25 cents.

Includes information on State and regional industrial directories published by State agencies and private organizations.

Director listings show title, latest date of issue, name of sponsoring organization, price, and symbols indicating type and arrangement of data contained.

A FINAL WORD . . .

Well, there it is. Obviously, I could go on and on. Books on art, books on music . . . did you know that the Navy publishes a *Hymnal* and a book on music theory?

You can win many a bet by convincing your open-mouthed friends that they can't name a subject, from A to Z, from the cradle to the grave, from athlete's foot to space travel, on which Uncle Sam hasn't published some useful information!

How can any American survey this treasure-trove without feeling a surge of love and pride, without voicing a silent prayer of humble thanks for the privilege of being part of a nation truly "of the people, by the people, and for the people."